WORKING
PARENTS
SURVIVAL
HANDBOOK

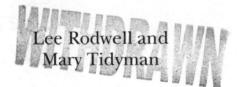

Lee Rodwell and
Mary Tidyman

075 210 2486

This book is dedicated to our mothers, Olive Rodwell and Peggy McKie, who showed it could be done, and to our children Tamsin, Guy, Annie, Polly and Tom for helping to make it work.

Acknowledgements

We would like to acknowledge Lisa Harker of the Daycare Trust for her useful comments and suggestions; the Maternity Alliance for help in preparing the sections on pregnancy rights; Parents at Work and Gillian Stellman, on NCT teacher. For general advice and willing interviewers; the Health Visitors Association; the Association for Postnatal Illness; MAMA; Carol Cooper; and Kate Woodward-Hay.

Published in 1995
Health Education Authority Books
Hamilton House
Mabledon Place
London WC1H 9TX

© Lee Rodwell and Mary Tidyman
ISBN 0 7521 0248 6

A CIP Catalogue record for this book is available from the British Library.

Typesetting by DP Photosetting, Aylesbury, Bucks
Printed in Great Britain by Biddles, Guildford, Surrey

CONTENTS

INTRODUCTION

The Working Parents Survival Handbook has been written to help parents with one of the most demanding phases in their lives – bringing up young children while continuing to work. This handbook is packed with practical ideas for dealing with the day-to-day concerns that you may face. It's intended as a guide to dip into rather than to be read from cover to cover, to help you with the issues or decisions that are relevant to you at a particular stage.

Your needs and problems will not remain static. The perfect solution to your childcare needs at one time may be quite inappropriate as children move from pre-school to school, or a second child is born; what you look for from a job may evolve and change with time; and finding ways to enjoy time with your children will alter as those children get older and develop different needs and interests.

WHO THE BOOK IS FOR

True, on the whole it is mothers who take the responsibility for looking after children, or organising alternative childcare if they work, and this book offers practical help for women who are juggling work and parenting. However, fathers increasingly are playing an active role in parenting – both in day-to-day care and in the decisions concerning their children – and this book is for them too. As long as men are expected to channel themselves into work roles to the exclusion of their family commitments and personal development, they will miss out. Employers have a role to play here too, and we hope this book will enable them to gain some insight into ways to get the most from their workforce – the vast majority of whom will be parents – and how to develop family-friendly policies in order to tap into the valuable resource which parents offer the labour market.

Most people look for partners who, as well as enjoying an emotionally intimate relationship, will be supportive of their career or work roles and share the tasks involved with home and parenting. If both of you are in paid work, then when children arrive it can mean overload for one of you (usually mum) unless you both take on more responsibility. This doesn't mean everything has to be equally shared; it's fine to acknowledge that at any one time one of you may have a more demanding job, work longer hours in paid work, or be committed to training or career development. But there is still room for a shared approach to childcare and to problem-solving when new needs arise, and this book aims to help you work things out together.

Many people today find themselves bringing up children on their own and the help and information given throughout the book are very relevant to their needs too, with a particular chapter looking at work issues for lone parents.

WHAT DOES THE BOOK COVER?

Where parenting is concerned, there are no clear-cut rights and wrongs but rather different ways of meeting the challenges and finding ways to organise day-to-day life. The book does not attempt to tell you how to do things, but offers a range of different options from which to choose. What suits one family may be quite inappropriate for another. What's important is that you are able to find a way of organising things that works for you and in which you have confidence. Quotes and case studies are included to bring the information to life, and to present a huge range of different approaches and solutions that have worked for other parents.

No book can cover every possible issue or provide all the answers, so information about some useful organisations is provided at the end of the book, together with a comprehensive index to signpost you to relevant topics.

Because the great majority of child carers are women, we have referred to them throughout as such. For variety, children have been referred to as 'he' or 'she' at random.

WHY WORK?

Many parents work because they have to. For some couples, financial commitments may make it difficult to cope on one income, and for the growing number of lone parents paid work may be a way of achieving a better standard of living.

Other parents may choose to work. While some parents enjoy and get fulfilment from caring for their children full-time, others may find that being a non-stop parent leaves them feeling depressed, trapped or undervalued. A job can provide contact with other adults to help keep you sane, and be a boost to your self-esteem and confidence. You may even find your overall health benefits, and you will probably enjoy the greater financial independence you have.

"Our son might be better off if one of us stayed home with him. But we are more fulfilled and content because we work, and that will benefit him in the long run."

David (30) banker

If you're lucky, your work may provide an interesting challenge in a chosen field, and be more than just a way to earn a living. Keeping a foot in the door may be important for long-term career prospects. Taking time off while children are young may mean that when you're ready to go back to work your skills need updating or you have to settle for a job several rungs down the ladder.

Your children may benefit too from you working. There is no evidence to show that children are better off being cared for exclusively by their parents. Spending time in a job that challenges and interests you can leave you with more energy rather than less to enjoy time with your children. Even mundane jobs may provide a change of routine that means you appreciate your children more when you're with them. As children get older, they may enjoy the extra money that your job brings in – perhaps funding some of their treats, clothes and holidays. Being introduced to a variety of other people and situations and a range of interesting activities and experiences may well help develop their confidence with other children and adults, and broaden their view of the world.

How your own parents integrated work and family responsibilities will have affected the vision you have for yourself. Your children will learn a great deal about work and family life by observing and interacting with you. The roles you and your partner play in day-to-day parenting and household tasks, whether you seem satisfied with the choices you've made and provide experiences that broaden or narrow their view of life will affect what your children see as possible for themselves. Less stereotyped gender roles within your family may encourage daughters to have greater confidence in their abilities and aspirations, and sons to develop personal areas of their life beyond just work.

One of the keys to combining successful parenting and employment is good planning and organisation – anticipating difficulties and organising things to get round them. Whatever your situation at home or work, it is possible to do a paid job well, enjoy life and be a good parent, and this book is intended to help you do just that.

1 PLANNING AHEAD

CHOOSING THE RIGHT SORT OF WORK

One of the factors you may consider when starting out in a particular area of work is how well you will be able to combine your job with raising a family at some point in the future. You no longer have to choose between career and parenthood. It is possible for both you and your partner, if you have one, to find fulfilment from work while at the same time sharing the responsibilities of home and children. Some jobs are just better suited than others to being combined with looking after a home and children. Think about these points:

- Will the job be amenable to flexible working, or can you organise your own time to some extent?
- Will the job require you to put in long or unpredictable hours?
- Will your skills become outdated quickly, or will it be easy to pick up where you leave off or update with a refresher course?
- Will it be easy to take a break from your job without damaging your long-term prospects?
- Will you have to work shifts or rotas? These may be hard to manage because your childcare needs will constantly change.
- Will your work take you away from home? This may be more stressful for your children, and more difficult to organise unless you have live-in help.
- Will the job help you develop skills and experience which are easy to exploit on a freelance basis?
- Are there plenty of temporary jobs available to give you a way back into work?

- Are you likely to be able to find an employer offering innovative, family-friendly policies? (See below.)

FAMILY-FRIENDLY EMPLOYERS

The success of an organisation depends to a great extent on having skilled and well-motivated employees, and using them to their full potential. Many employers are waking up to the fact that it is in their interest to retain their female workers. If you're valued at work, your employer faces losing all your experience and knowledge if you leave and will have to meet the cost of finding a replacement for you. In most cases it makes more sense to find a way of holding on to you through incentives and enticements.

There are several initiatives that an employer can offer to make it easier for a woman to return to work after having a baby, and to help both mothers and fathers combine their work and family commitments. A growing number of employers from both the public and private sectors, large firms and small, are looking again at their employment policies and finding innovative ways to make the most of their workforce by enabling parents to balance their paid work and family responsibilities. Banks, retail chains and the NHS, for example, are finding that schemes such as flexible working patterns, and workplace nurseries are encouraging a high proportion of their female staff to return to work after maternity leave. It's by no means universal, and there is still a lot of progress to be made, but the following types of initiative illustrate the good practice that is springing up around the country:

- **Maternity leave** in excess of statutory – up to a year's leave.
- **Maternity pay** in excess of statutory.
- **Adoptive parents leave** – may offer extended paid leave for adoptive parents on adoption of a child of pre-school age.

- **Paternity leave** – a fixed number of days' paid leave in any one calendar year for birth and adoption.
- **Keep-in-touch scheme** – women on maternity leave are given the opportunity of attending staff meetings, training sessions and other relevant events to update their skills and help them keep up-to-date with the organisation.
- **Flexible working patterns** – including flexi-time, home working, job-sharing, part-time and term-time working.
  - **Job-sharing** – ideally, all posts should be available for job-share; if the best candidate for the post wishes to take it on a job-share basis and no other good candidate has requested job-share, the second half of the post will be readvertised.
  - **Flexi-time** – there are core times when staff are expected to be at work; other than this, all hours up to 6.30 pm are considered, and hours worked in excess of 37 per week may be taken off as flexi- days. Flexi-time may, for example, enable you to take your child to school before starting work in the morning.
- **Childcare information and referral service.**
- **Childcare subsidy** – providing childcare vouchers for parents (both men and women) can help to offset the huge cost involved in alternative childcare when both parents work. This may be offered to all staff irrespective of grade, or targeted at the lower paid or certain priority groups such as lone parents. Subsidies vary, but may be £25 per week, or 50 per cent of costs, whichever is the lowest, available for each pre-school child. Usually only children up to five years are eligible.
- **A range of childcare facilities**, including on-site nursery/crèche, near-site provision in partnership with other local providers at a subsidised rate, after-school initiatives, childminders' network offering high quality, affordable and

flexible childcare close to home with back-up cover if child-minder is ill.

- **Holiday and out-of-school playschemes** – for children of five years and upwards, on a full-time, part-time or occasional basis after school and throughout the school holidays. A range of sporting, arts and crafts activities are available, with qualified staff to supervise children at all times.
- **Sick child leave** – discretionary paid leave to care for a sick child.
- **Returners' training** – distance learning and springboard options covering a range of vocational and developmental courses; reimbursement of childcare expenses resulting from training.
- **Pro-rata full-time benefits for part-time workers.**

You may already be in a job that fits in marvellously with the demands of parenting. If so, that's great. If not, you could try negotiating with your employer for a more flexible work pattern. Whether or not you feel able to ask will probably depend on how secure you feel at work.

WHEN'S THE RIGHT TIME TO HAVE CHILDREN?

Is there ever a right time to have a baby? If you actually sit down and think about it, there are probably lots of things you will want to consider. Deciding when to have a baby is a very personal decision based on your own particular feelings and circumstances. How old you are may be one factor. A woman's fertility starts to decline after the age of 30, going steadily downhill from mid-30s onwards. Should you have a child while you're young and fit, flexible enough to accommodate the demands that children will make on your life, and so that if you do have problems becoming pregnant you have plenty of time to do something about them? Do you and your partner feel ready for the commitment and responsibility of children, or should you wait until you're more mature and experienced in life? What about spaces between children? Is it best to have them close together and get all the nappies and sleepless nights out of the way quickly, or plan larger gaps and have a less frantic existence and time to give them more individual attention?

Your work situation will be one of the considerations that you'll want to put into the equation when weighing up the best time to start a family. Pregnancy is bound to have some impact on your job – even if you intend to return to work soon after the birth, you will need to take some maternity leave, and life will never be quite the same again! If you've been in your present job a short time and haven't yet established a good track record, you may feel vulnerable. Your length of service will affect your maternity rights, although from October 1994 all women are entitled to 14 weeks' maternity leave and paid time off for antenatal care, no matter how long they have been in their job or how many hours they work, and it is illegal to dismiss or make any woman redundant because she is pregnant (see 'Your rights at work', page 68).

More and more couples, especially those in professional careers, are delaying parenthood until the woman reaches her 30s. You may want to wait until you've completed your training and got some experience, feel more secure financially, and are established in a position where it will be easier to return after a break. If you're worried that your chances of promotion will be damaged by taking time off to have a child, remember that on your return your employer must offer you a job at least equivalent to your existing one, and there is nothing to stop you applying for more senior positions that become vacant while you're on leave. If you have a very responsible position you may be concerned that things will be mismanaged while you're away – there may be some periods when it's easier to take a break without too much disruption at work.

If you've been working in a job that hasn't allowed you to develop your full potential up to now, you may be considering a change of direction or rethinking your career. Some people find it useful to combine this with taking some time off from paid work to start a family. Part-time courses, open learning modules and the like may be a feasible way of skilling yourself or working towards a qualification and maintaining some mental stimulation while caring for young children. This way, by the time you're ready to go back to work, you will have some new skills to offer and a wider range of work opportunities available to you.

You may also want to consider your partner's work situation when planning a pregnancy. You will need some extra support and attention during pregnancy, and a new baby will make demands on both of you, so it's best to avoid a period when your partner has extra work commitments such as having to work very long hours or be away from home more than usual. The policies of your partner's employer towards issues such as paternity leave and flexible working arrangements may well be something to consider when deciding if the time is right to have a baby (see 'Family-friendly employers', page 7).

WHEN THINGS DON'T GO TO PLAN

Of course, it's not always possible to start a family to order because despite advances in our understanding of reproductive processes, babies do not always come according to plan. It may take you a while to conceive once you start trying, or alternatively you may find yourself with a pregnancy you didn't plan.

"I'd got it all worked out so that my maternity leave would coincide with term-times to give me the maximum amount of time off with the baby. Unfortunately, I had a miscarriage and next time round the timing didn't work out quite so well."

Jill (29) teacher

FERTILITY PROBLEMS

It may seem like the cruellest trick in the book. You spend years trying to avoid pregnancy, only to find when you feel ready to start a family that you can't conceive to order. This can leave you feeling vulnerable and out of control. It can be very unsettling, not knowing from one month to the next if you're going to get pregnant, and therefore being unable to plan far ahead. Do you decide to change jobs at this stage, with the risk that if you do get pregnant you may not qualify for full maternity benefits? Should you put yourself forward for promotion when actually your work is not getting your full attention? Or do you put your life and your work on hold while you try to sort out what is probably the most preoccupying issue on your mind?

The problem with infertility is that you are unlikely to get any speedy and definite answers. You may have to wait quite a while before your doctor will even begin to explore your situation – couples are often advised to try for a baby for up to two years before taking any further action to find out if anything is wrong, and what to do about it. You may want to talk to your boss or personnel manager and put them in the picture so they understand your situation and can make allowances, for example, if you have to go for treatment over a lengthy period of time. On the other hand, you may be reluctant to share what is after all a very personal problem, and worry that you are putting your position in jeopardy by being so open. Only you can judge what is your best course of action, based on your situation and the attitude of people at work.

FOSTERING AND ADOPTION

For people who want to foster or adopt a child, there can also be work-related problems. The lengthy procedures involved in becoming accepted for adoption will probably mean you and your partner need to take time off work. It can be a very stressful experience, making it difficult to concentrate on other things in your life – including work! If you are accepted, you may then have to wait some time for a 'suitable' child to become available, and again this will be beyond your control. Whereas biological parents get up to nine months' warning of their impending parenthood, people who foster or adopt a child may get very little notice.

"It was strange really but I got the news that we'd been accepted for adoption the same day that I got promotion at work. It was very bewildering and I wasn't sure what to do for the best. I decided to explain at work about the adoption and turn down the promotion because I thought I'd want to give up work once a baby became available for us. My boss turned out to be very understanding and insisted the promotion went ahead. I was in my new post for three months before our daughter was placed with us. I was then offered adoptive parents' leave that was the same length and conditions as my company's normal maternity leave.

After six months' leave, I decided to go back to work part-time."

Felicity (35) accounts manager

WHEN PREGNANCY AND WORK CONFLICT

Many pregnancies are unplanned in the sense that they don't happen exactly when expected. Sometimes, a pregnancy occurs at a time that is difficult as far as work is concerned – for example, when you've just taken on more responsibility, several other key people you work with are also on leave, or you've been seconded to go on a training programme. It may help to think through your options:

- **Put your career on hold and throw yourself into parenting;** you can keep your options open at work and see if you want to go back once your maternity leave runs out (see 'Going back to work' on page 62).
- **Defer your training or career development plans** until you feel ready to tackle them.
- **Look at ways of adapting your work** to make it easier to combine with parenting – e.g. by reducing your hours or working from home for a while.
- **Share childcare responsibilities with your partner** – perhaps they could take a career break now if it's not a good time for you.

"I was dismayed to find myself pregnant again, having just taken up a demanding job after several years' break looking after my two sons. Having thought through all the possibilities, I decided to take just three months' leave and return to work full-time. I managed to get a place for the baby in my workplace nursery. Having her cared for on-site meant I could carry on breastfeeding, and we all adjusted to the new situation very well. Despite several months of sleepless nights, I don't honestly think my work suffered!"

Fiona (33) university lecturer

2 BREAKING THE NEWS AT WORK

WHEN TO SHARE THE GOOD NEWS

One of the first decisions facing any working parent has to be made before your child is even born: when to tell employers and colleagues that a baby is on the way.

THE LEGAL REQUIREMENTS

From the working mother's point of view there are several different factors that may influence the timing. If you plan to take maternity leave and want to safeguard your right to return to work you will have to let your employer know officially at some point: the exact date depends on when you plan to start your leave.

The earliest maternity leave can begin is 11 weeks before your baby is due. However, you can work right up to the last week. Whatever date you choose, you must inform your employers, in writing, at least three weeks in advance. (For detailed information, see page 61.)

Whether you break the news before this is up to you. Some women are so excited by the prospect of having a baby that they want to share their joy as soon as the pregnancy test shows positive. Others prefer to keep their secret until people start to comment on the fact that they seem to be putting on weight. Only you can judge what seems best in your circumstances, but it's worth bearing in mind the following points.

THE REACTION OF COLLEAGUES

Although legally you can't be sacked for becoming pregnant, the news that you are expecting a baby will be greeted differently, depending on a variety of factors. For example, if the company you work for is used to arranging cover for employees taking maternity leave, your pregnancy is more likely to be greeted with congratulations than ill-disguised irritation at the disruption your absence might cause.

You might be asked about your intentions, whether you intend to leave work altogether, whether you plan to take maternity leave, when you want this to start. Yet you might not be clear in your own mind about the course of action you want to take, and it is important not to be pressured into making any decisions until you are ready.

The early months of pregnancy may not be easy as your body is undergoing all kinds of changes and you may feel far from your normal self, although outwardly you'll probably look much the same as usual. You might feel it would be helpful if those around you knew what was happening, too.

THE RISK OF MISCARRIAGE

Even so, many women prefer to wait a while. Miscarriages are quite common in the first 12 weeks of pregnancy and can be very upsetting. If this was to happen to you, you might find things even more distressing if you had to keep on explaining what had happened to people at work because they already knew about your pregnancy.

"I was offered promotion a week after I learned I was pregnant. I felt it was only fair to tell the company that I would be needing some maternity leave if I took the post. They were fine about it, so I

started work in a new department where everyone knew about the baby.

But a month later I had a miscarriage and for some weeks afterwards I had to go through the painful (for me) and embarrassing (for them) task of explaining this to work-mates who knew I'd been expecting a baby, but not that I'd lost it. The next time I was pregnant I kept quiet about it until I was well past the early weeks."

Sandra (32) picture researcher

There is no evidence to show that working can in itself cause a miscarriage although there are some jobs that may pose health hazards for pregnant women (see page 50). However, if you threaten to miscarry (that is, if you have vaginal bleeding that may or may not be accompanied by pain) your doctor will probably advise you to stop work and stay in bed until the bleeding stops.

Even then you may not feel it is necessary to tell your employer the exact reason for your absence. You could say you had gynaecological problems or just stomach pains.

"I told them I'd had abdominal pains which was the truth, if not the whole truth, and let them assume it was a stomach upset. The problem was that we had just been taken over by another firm and I didn't want the new management to get the impression that I might be leaving at any time.

It was possible I might never have a baby and might be working there for another ten years. I didn't want them to start making any assumptions that might have affected my partnership prospects until I knew myself which way my future would pan out. In the end I didn't tell anyone – including my mother – that I was pregnant until I was well past the four months stage."

Penny (33) solicitor

THE NEED FOR INFORMATION

Another factor that may affect the timing of announcement could well be your need for more information. You will have to establish what you will be entitled to in terms of maternity rights and benefits. It's possible that you were given all the necessary details when you first started your job, as part of your contract or in the basic terms and conditions of your employment. You may know where to look for the information if it is contained in the company handbook.

The legal minimum entitlements are covered later in this book, but your employer may have a better in-house deal. If there is a trade union where you work, you should be able to get details from your representative about the maternity package on offer. If you don't have a union you will have to approach your boss or personnel department for the information you need. Of course, you don't have to say that you are pregnant, but clearly such a request can be cause for speculation.

Another reason why you might have to let people know you are pregnant sooner, rather than later, would be if the work you do might pose a health risk to you or your baby. Employers have a duty of care – but until your employer knows you are pregnant, any necessary measures to safeguard your health can't be taken. The kind of things which might affect you are discussed in more detail later in this chapter.

HOW TO BREAK THE NEWS

To some extent the way you officially announce your pregnancy will depend on the amount of information you already have and your plans for the future. That said, it is better to break the news in a business-like manner, rather than bursting into tears one day and announcing that it's all too much because you're pregnant!

You could write a short letter or make an appointment to see your immediate boss in person. Either way, it is better if your employer hears the news from you, rather than via the workplace grapevine. Depending on the structure of your organisation, you may end up dealing solely with your boss, or you may have to see his or her superior, or the personnel department.

KEEP YOUR OPTIONS OPEN

Make up your mind beforehand how much information you want to give or get at this stage. Even if you are feeling ambivalent about how your work will fit into your future plans it is important not to say anything that could be taken to mean you are going to give up your job or leave permanently. You should make sure you keep all your options open.

If you are seeing your employer face to face, practise what you are going to say. For example, "I've come to tell you that I'm expecting a baby on (date baby is due) and I will let you know in due course when I will be starting my maternity leave."

You may be asked to commit yourself to specific dates regarding the start and finish of your maternity leave. Providing there is still enough time for you to give at least three weeks' notice of the date you intend to start your leave, you are not obliged to make any final decisions at this stage. So if you are not sure yet, and you've got time to think about it, resist any pressure to commit yourself to anything.

Remember, the way you feel now about work and about the baby may not be the same in a few months' time. So you need to keep a flexible approach to make sure you do not lose any of your rights.

Assertiveness skills can come in handy (more about these below). You can acknowledge what the other person says without giving your ground. For example,

'I appreciate that:

- you would like to know when I will be stopping work;
- you need to know when to advertise for someone to cover;
- you will find it difficult to manage without me;
- you would rather I was back at work before the Christmas rush.

And I will:

- let you know what I have decided as soon as I can;
- give you the details in writing when I have thought a little more about it.'

ASSERTIVENESS

As a working parent you will often find yourself having to negotiate at home and at work. You may want to change your hours of work, or you may want more help with the chores at home. You may want to ask the person caring for your child to do something your way, rather than theirs.

If you find this kind of situation difficult, or if you never seem to come away with a satisfactory result, learning some assertiveness skills may make all the difference. People who teach these skills say they aim to foster the art of clear, honest and direct communication.

Assertiveness means recognising that you are valuable in your own right, and that your needs and desires are valid. Being assertive allows you to stand up for your rights and act in your own best interests while also respecting the rights and feelings of others. It is very different from aggressive behaviour, when you try to get what you want regardless of the other people's needs or feelings.

Most assertiveness trainers suggest people begin by reminding themselves of some basic rights we all have. Acknowledging you have these rights will help you to think assertively.

Your charter of rights

I have the right to:

- state my own needs
- set my own priorities
- be treated with respect as a capable, intelligent equal
- express my feelings
- express my opinions
- say yes – or no – without feeling guilty
- lead my life without depending on other people's approval
- refuse responsibility for other people's problems
- change my mind
- make mistakes
- say I don't understand and ask for information
- make time for myself

NEGOTIATE FOR A BETTER DEAL

Some companies offer only the legal minimum when it comes to maternity leave and pay. Others offer better packages. If you don't already know what you are likely to be entitled to, now is the time to ask. You should ask "Could you let me have all the information about the maternity package this company offers?"

Once you know what rights and benefits you are entitled to, you might want to consider negotiating for a better deal.

Think about your job as a package. What else do you get besides your salary? Do you get any of the things listed in the checklist below?

Checklist	Yes	No
Company car	☐	☐
Private health care	☐	☐
Staff discounts	☐	☐
Pension	☐	☐
Cheap loans	☐	☐
Training courses	☐	☐
Health club membership	☐	☐
Mortgage subsidies	☐	☐
Paid holidays	☐	☐

If your company has its own maternity package, check to see what, if any, of these things are covered. Companies vary a great deal in what they allow women to keep when they are on maternity leave. During the 14 weeks general maternity leave period, to which all women are now entitled, your 'contractual rights' continue. This means, for example, that if you are entitled to a company car you have the right to keep it during this time, and your holiday entitlement will continue to accrue.

However, if you qualify for a longer period of leave, your rights are not explicitly protected by law beyond those 14 weeks. You might want to negotiate with your employers to see if they will agree to you claiming your full holiday entitlement during your maternity leave. If you have difficulty you could get further advice from your trade union, the local Citizens' Advice Bureau or a law centre, to help you argue your case

Even when it comes down to the basic things like the length of maternity leave and the amount of paid time off, some companies offer deals that are better than the legal minimums. For example:

- Some top up the 18 weeks' statutory maternity pay;
- Some extend the period of paid leave;
- Some give an extended period of maternity leave so that a woman has a right to return to her job well past the statutory minimum of 29 weeks after the birth;
- Some agree to keep women on maternity leave informed of events taking place at work;
- Some give them the right to be consulted over any job changes and to be considered for training;
- Some allow women to return to work on reduced hours to begin with.

Action checklist

- If there are any other women in your organisation who have taken maternity leave, it may pay to compare notes with them to see what kind of deal they got.
- Take advice from your trade union rep if you have one. The TUC also publish a useful Guide to Maternity Rights and Benefits. Your library may have a copy.
- Keep copies of any correspondence and notes of any conversations. In particular, if you are offered anything above and beyond the standard maternity package make sure you get the offer in writing.
- It is also worth making it clear that you still want to be considered for any training or promotion that may interest you and would like to be sent company newsletters, reports and other information relevant to your job while you are on leave.

WORKING FATHERS

Fathers have no legal rights to paternity leave or to time off to accompany their partner to antenatal appointments or classes. That said, a growing number of companies now offer their staff a relatively short period of paternity leave at around the time of the birth. In addition men often informally arrange to take a day off from time to time, to attend antenatal clinics with their partner.

Even so, because fathers do not have the same kind of rights as mothers, men are sometimes hesitant about letting their employers and colleagues know that a baby is expected. This is often because men are afraid of what their employer will think. They fear that they may be seen as less committed or less flexible, and so they may try to play down the stresses and strains that can surface throughout their partner's pregnancy and continue after the birth.

However, management consultant Rodger O'Connell, who runs workshops for fathers, argues that the lack of specific rights makes it even more important to open a dialogue with employers about the change in your circumstances sooner rather than later.

And as he points out, being there for the first scan, or going to 'couples' classes to prepare for the labour and birth, are ways of involving yourself with the baby from the very early days. "If the baby arrives, and that is your first point of contact, you will have a lot of catching up to do," he says.

Most men will have to negotiate to take time off. Without any legal minimum as a starting point, you may feel in a weak position. It is a good idea to think about what you want, and to get that in perspective in relation to what you put in.

You may want some time off during your partner's pregnancy. You may want a couple of days off around the estimated time of the birth, followed by another week or so after the baby has arrived. In the first few weeks you might want to be sure you can go home on time. You might not want to be sent away on business for the first month or so.

Once you know what you are likely to be asking for, ask yourself how long you have been in the job, and how long you expect to stay there. Seen in that light, a request for leave or a temporary change in your work arrangements may feel far more reasonable.

After all, at senior levels in many companies men are sent on training courses that take them out of the office for days at a time. Their absence is allowed, even encouraged, because they are felt to be acquiring better skills that will benefit the company. Yet the same argument can be applied to paternity leave. Becoming a parent involves managing change and learning to be flexible – and both are skills which employers value. In addition, research has shown that having a happy domestic environment encourages a good performance at work. Stress on the home front has the reverse effect.

The next stage is to find out how your employer feels. If you don't talk openly about the situation you lose the opportunity to plan ahead and influence events that are going to happen anyway. It is better to acknowledge that there will be changes in your life and to discuss the implications.

Finally, try to come up with some proposals that will suit both you, your employer, and your colleagues. These could involve taking extended unpaid leave, being able to leave on time, not having to go away on trips, switching to a different role in the organisation, even taking most of your holiday entitlement all at once. The more flexible your proposals, the more likely you are to be able to reach a compromise that works for you, your family and your company.

"I worked long hours and was often away travelling in the UK and across Europe. I approached my boss and sounded him out about a more flexible arrangement once the baby was born. I was pleasantly surprised at how supportive he was. We came up with various ideas but I ended up effectively working part-time for three months. I turn up according to the business needs – they might need me just one day one week, and four or five days the next. The only control is that it has to balance out at 50 per cent of a normal working week. It's worked very well."

Martin (35) management consultant

Negotiation checklist

What do I want? Time off to go to clinics/ to be at the birth/ to be with my newborn/ to be able to go home on time/ not to be sent away on trips for a while.

What does my employer think about this? Ask for information/ reaction.

Make a proposal. Unpaid leave/work from home for a while/ switch to tasks that mean regular hours

---

WHEN TO STOP WORK

FINANCES

You will inevitably have to weigh up a number of different factors when trying to decide when it will be best to stop working. One of these will be financial. Even if you qualify for maternity pay rather than maternity allowance, it will be less than you could earn unless your employer is offering more than the legal minimum. In addition, if you are going to take the maximum leave of 29 weeks after the birth of the baby it might seem best to work on as late as possible, say until two weeks before the baby is due. With 18 weeks SMP (Statutory Maternity Pay) to come you would be at home, unpaid, for fewer weeks.

On the other hand, some childbirth educators are concerned at the trend for women to work so late into pregnancy that they do not leave themselves enough time to get ready for the birth.

Whatever your plans, make sure you know what you are entitled to. Since October 1994 it is no longer true that you will lose any SMP if you work during the last six weeks before the baby is due.

PEOPLE AT WORK

The attitudes of those you work for and with may also need to be taken into consideration. If they have been supportive you are less likely to feel like stopping work at the earliest possible time than if they have been ambivalent or even hostile.

Women report that attitudes vary enormously, even between different branches of the same organisation. Sometimes colleagues go out of their way to be helpful; sometimes they can be extremely thoughtless. And sometimes it is not colleagues' unwillingness to help that is a problem, but the lack of enough staff to do so.

There are also times when employers add to the pressures by expecting women not only to handle their routine work, but to train a successor or complete projects before going off on maternity leave. On the other hand, some women find themselves with less to do because, they feel, their employers have decided to 'side-line' them during their period of pregnancy and maternity leave.

"I was allowed to do a job that enabled me to sit down for most of the time."

Pam (28) bank clerk

"A little more consideration would have been welcome. Lifting and carrying were the most worrying aspects as I was involved with loading and unloading a cash dispenser. When no one was available to help I was expected to cope alone. I was also expected to cover many jobs without assistance. Most people think this job is a sedentary one, but on the contrary you are up and down all the time, answering queries from customers, seeing to the computer and so on."

Rina (27) bank clerk

"Overall the concern of my colleagues was touching but there was actually more work to do – special projects were brought forward so that I could do them before I left."

Therese (33) specialist clerk in an American-owned bank

"I made it plain I was coming back to work after the baby. But once I'd announced my pregnancy no new accounts came my way. Officially I was told it was just in case I found the workload too much and they also felt it was better continuity if someone else, who wasn't going to be away for three months, took the work on. But since the firm wasn't noted for its altruism I doubt very much whether they were really concerned about my welfare."

Jaqui (34) public relations consultant.

Rather than feeling pressured into stopping work because of the attitudes of others it may be worth trying to see if you can solve some of the difficulties first. Obviously, if you have a good working relationship with your employer and colleagues, they are more likely to be considerate during your pregnancy. Even so, if they have no experience of pregnancy themselves, they may not realise difficulties exist unless you tell them.

What you can do

- Consider talking over the situation with your employer and/ or your colleagues.
- Instead of issuing an ultimatum, offer a possible solution: employers by and large do not relish having to deal with any more problems than they already face in an average day.

  Would it help if you could:
  - swap tasks with someone else;
  - work from home, at least part of the time;
  - start and finish work earlier or later?

  Would a few changes in the workplace make a difference:
  - an electric fan to keep you cooler;
  - a better chair to ease your backache?
- Maintain a business-like attitude and let people know you are not just marking time until you can collect your maternity pay – your job is still important.

PRESSURES ON THE HOME FRONT

Even if everything is going smoothly at work, some women find they are under pressure from their partner or other family members to stop work sooner rather than later. This may be because they are genuinely concerned about the wisdom of working on through pregnancy – but there may be other reasons, too.

In the past, women often gave up their jobs almost as soon as they knew they were pregnant. This signalled the start of a new phase of their lives as homemakers and childcarers. The pattern of women's lives may now have changed, but people still have a tendency to expect others to behave the way they did when they were younger. So your mother or your mother-in-law may have firm views about your working.

"My mother-in-law told me I was being thoughtless to carry on working. She implied I didn't care about the baby, that people would think her son couldn't earn enough to support us. She couldn't understand why I wanted to work when I could have stayed at home getting the baby's room ready."

Anna (28) buyer

Your partner may also have different views from you. In an ideal world we would all sit down at the start of a relationship and discuss our hopes and expectations. In practice, a lot of our feelings stay undefined and undisclosed, only surfacing when something – such as pregnancy – changes our lives. Often these feelings are linked to the way we were brought up, the way our own family behaved.

"I'd assumed I'd work as long as possible, take maternity leave and go back when the baby was about six months old. But when I said something about it to my husband not long after we found out I was pregnant, I realised he wanted me to stop work at about 28 weeks and stay at home until the baby was much older. He didn't understand how important my job was to me, or how I could possibly think about what I wanted as well as what would be best for the baby. Of course, his mother gave up work when she fell pregnant with his older sister, and never worked again."

Louise (31) journalist

"When I found out I was pregnant I was really happy and started to make plans about leaving work. But my husband said there was no reason for me not to carry on – in fact, he thought we should both go on earning as long as possible. But we didn't desperately need the money and I didn't much like the job I was in anyway."

Christine (33) accountant

As far as partners go, it is essential to talk things through and, if necessary, come to some kind of compromise which you both feel happy with. If you are going to bring up a child together you need to find a way of reaching joint decisions right from the start.

As to other family members:

- avoid getting drawn into arguments;
- explain your plans, politely but firmly, and refuse to discuss the situation further;
- try to let any pointed comments wash over you;
- if that's impossible, consider cutting down the amount of time you spend with people who can't or won't see your point of view;
- remember, babies have a way of mending bridges when they arrive – and, after all, it is your life. You must decide how to run it.

COMPLICATIONS OF PREGNANCY

Unfortunately, if you develop complications during your pregnancy, all you carefully laid plans about when to stop work may be thrown into disarray. If your blood pressure rises significantly you may be told to stay at home in bed, since hypertension can be a warning sign of pre-eclampsia, a condition that, if left untreated, can be dangerous for you and your baby. If you start bleeding after 27 weeks this may be a sign that part of the placenta has peeled away from the uterus. Again, bed-rest will be prescribed.

If you go into premature labour you may be admitted to hospital to see if the contractions can be stopped.

Before you reach the last six weeks of your pregnancy, you can take sick leave for a pregnancy-related illness without affecting your maternity leave or pay. Once you reach this point, however, you are no longer entitled to claim Statutory Sick Pay, unless your illness has nothing to do with the pregnancy. Instead you will be put straight on to maternity leave by your employer who will then start paying you maternity pay.

MAKING UP YOUR MIND

In many ways, pregnancy can be as unpredictable as childbirth itself. Thinking about the issues involved in working through pregnancy can help you work out what your ideal plan would be, but in the end, you must be prepared to adapt and change according to circumstances, just as you will have to adapt and change throughout the period of your life when you are a working parent.

And it is important to remind yourself that you don't have to have everything planned right at the start when you won't know what to expect physically or emotionally.

You may find the first three months, coping with tiredness and nausea, the worst of all. Or you may sail through the early stages only to find the thought of heaving your increasing bulk on to another crowded bus too much to face towards the end. You may change your mind several times about how you want to balance work and parenthood. Your feelings about everything may change from one month to the next.

Ultimately, only you can know all the factors involved in deciding when to stop work. But the following checklist of things to think about might help you come to a decision.

Checklist

- How tired is my job making me?
- How much support will I get at work if I carry on?
- How much support am I getting at home?
- Is my doctor happy for me to go on working?
- If I stopped now, would worrying about money be more of a strain than staying at work?
- Am I still enjoying my work?
- Would I miss my colleagues if I was at home?
- Do I feel on top of the job?
- Do I feel I'm leaving enough time to get ready for the baby?

Perhaps the best advice is simply to think about what your work involves and what your priorities are. Make your plans, but in the end listen to what your body tells you. As Professor Geoffrey Chamberlain, president of the Royal College of Obstetricians and Gynaecologists, says: "If you enjoy your job and take sensible steps to make sure you do not overstretch yourself, then there is no reason for you to give it up. Many women are so much more conscious of their body and its needs that they know when it is time to stop or reduce the levels of work."

3 LOOKING AFTER YOURSELF

KEEPING WELL

COPING WITH TIREDNESS

One of the most common symptoms of early pregnancy is tiredness. Even if your working day has been relatively easy you may still find yourself feeling absolutely exhausted in the evenings. The feeling of lethargy may persist through the day, too, during the first three months. Doctors suggest that this lack of energy is frequently associated with a fall in blood pressure as a result of hormonal changes. This may be the body's way of ensuring a woman rests during the time when so many crucial foetal developments are taking place.

- **Sort out your priorities.** Does it really matter if you become a social recluse for a few weeks? Go to bed early if you find yourself falling asleep on the sofa. Have a lie-in at weekends. Use your lunch-hour to rest instead of shopping or going out with your friends.
- **Rest when you can.** Find out if there is a first-aid room or a conference room a work where you can lie down or put your feet up. Make the most of what is available. **It's worth knowing that employers now have a duty to provide 'suitable facilities ... for any person at work who is a pregnant woman or a nursing mother to rest.'** Any workplace used for the first time after the end of 1992 must already comply with this regulation. Older workplaces have until the end of 1995 to comply.

- **Try to avoid travelling during rush hours.** If you work for a company that has flexible working hours you may be able to make the journeys to and from work during less crowded times. Even if no such system operates it may be worth finding out whether you could go in earlier – or later – to avoid rush hour. Stand up for your right to sit down – if someone is sitting in one of those 'reserved for...' seats, ask them if they'd mind getting up. Explain that you are pregnant. Most people are happy to co-operate.
- **Consider ways you might reorganise your workload.** Some aspects of your job may be particularly tiring – for example, if you are on your feet a lot, or having to lift and carry bulky objects. Are there times when you could sit instead of stand? Could you swap duties with anyone else? If you have the kind of job where you are preparing reports or dealing with paperwork would it be possible to work at home some days?
- **Seek more help at home.** Talking about the way you feel and the help you need is important. Outwardly, in the early days, you will still look much the same as usual, so unless you can explain to those around you just how tired you are, you are unlikely to get the support or sympathy you need at home.

If you are working as well as having a baby you will need time to rest. One way to get that time is to cut down on some of the household chores or to get someone else to do them. If you have a partner, you need to discuss the question of who now does what. If you have older children, now is the time to encourage them to help more, too. Can they make their own beds, load the washing machine, do the washing up?

If you can find someone to come in for just a couple of hours a week to do some ironing or cleaning it might be worth the expense. Work out how much help you need, what you can afford, and then try to find someone to fit the bill. The cheapest way is to put a card in the window of a local newsagent.

Many women are reluctant to ask for help with housework – let alone pay for it. But it is better to pay than to exhaust yourself. What is more important – personally getting the ring off the bath, or getting the rest you and your baby need?

- **Organise the chores.** List all the chores that need doing and the frequency with which they need to be done. Go back through the list and ask, 'is this really necessary?' If the answer is 'no', cross it off. Then go back through the list to see if any of the daily jobs could be done every other day, the weekly jobs every other week, and so on.

  Then think about the way you normally do some of the chores. Could you make them less tiring – iron sitting down, for example, or peel the potatoes sitting at the kitchen table with a bowl of water, rather than standing at the sink? Better still, have baked potatoes that need only a quick scrub.

- **Upgrade your household equipment.** If you can afford to, buying items like a microwave or a freezer can cut down on the time spent cooking or shopping for food. Dishwashers take the strain out of washing up. Tumble driers cut down the amount of ironing. All of these things will go on paying their way after the baby has arrived.

  If you haven't got the cash for big items, less expensive ones may also be time-savers. A non-stick pan can be washed up faster than a traditional one. Investing in a couple of sharp kitchen knives can speed up certain tasks, and lengthening the flex on the vacuum cleaner means you will not waste time and energy plugging and unplugging as you move from room to room.

"I was tired all the time in the early weeks of pregnancy. I didn't have the energy to cook much or to work with him in the garden. Just working full-time was about all I could cope with.

We'd always done things together and at first I think he resented the baby a little because it was coming between us. But once the pregnancy began to show and the baby became more real to him he was much more considerate and he took over quite a lot of the chores I'd done before."

Penny (23) receptionist

"I'd worked full-time and run the home for nine years, but during my pregnancy, when my husband realised how tired I was, he suggested we got a cleaning lady to come in for four hours a week. She was an absolute godsend and a real tonic."

Pam (37) office service supervisor

"I didn't blame people for not offering me a seat. After all, I didn't look pregnant. So I just used to say to someone, 'I wonder if I could sit down. You see, I'm pregnant and I'm feeling sick.' It always did the trick. Not only did I get a seat but people positively edged away!"

Lesley (41) supermarket supervisor

SICKNESS AND OTHER PROBLEMS DURING PREGNANCY

No one knows for certain why some women feel sick or are sick in pregnancy but it is estimated that up to 70 per cent of pregnant women suffer. Some simply feel mildly nauseous in the morning while others feel sick all day and vomit or retch frequently. If you were healthy and well nourished before you became pregnant, there is no evidence that being sick or unable to face food will cause any harm to the baby. However it can make life difficult for a working woman.

One of things that can exacerbate morning sickness is a long, tiring journey to work. But even if you can't improve your travelling conditions, there are some other things worth trying.

- Some doctors recommend increasing your intake of vitamin B6 so try eating foods high in this vitamin such as wholegrain cereals, wheatgerm, bananas or yeast extract

- Eating little but often, instead of sticking to three meals a day, may help you feel better.
- Increase your intake of complex carbohydrates, such as wholemeal bread, pasta, fresh fruit and vegetables and cut down on foods high in fat or protein. Avoid fried or fatty meals and choose chicken or fish instead of red meat.
- Try nibbling some dry toast or a plain biscuit before you sit up and get out of bed in the morning. Have a snack before you go to bed at night even if you don't feel like it. It may make you feel less sick the following morning. Sucking a boiled sweet may stop you being sick when you are travelling.
- Avoid clothes that feel tight around the waist. Fresh air and a short walk at lunchtime may help, too.
- If the sickness is really bad you should discuss the problem with your doctor who may prescribe a suitable drug. Some women have been helped by homeopathic remedies: the most commonly prescribed is ipecacuana, but there are others that may be more appropriate in individual cases. You can find out where your nearest homeopath is by contacting the British Homeopathic Association (see 'Addresses' on page 216).

Many women feel embarrassed if they have to keep disappearing to be sick. It may be best to explain to those around you what the problem is. Morning sickness is such a well-known symptom of pregnancy that bosses and colleagues are probably more likely to be sympathetic than anything else. If they aren't, only you can decide what the best course of action is. You may feel it is appropriate to point out that you are not doing this deliberately and you appreciate how inconvenient it is for everyone, not least yourself. You may decide to ignore the situation, on the grounds that you will soon be feeling better anyway. Or you may decide it is better to take time off sick, rather than trying to struggle on.

In fact, some women are so badly affected by sickness in their pregnancy that they have to take time off work. If this applies to you, there is no reason to feel guilty: people take time off for all kinds of health and family reasons. You wouldn't feel guilty if you were off work with gastric flu or a heavy cold because those are things beyond your control. In your case, so is your pregnancy sickness.

Having to keep dashing to the loo is another common symptom of early pregnancy that can be a nuisance at work. You will not solve this problem by drinking less. In fact, it is important to keep your fluid intake up, as during pregnancy there is a greater risk of urinary tract infection. The best thing is to plan your day so you are never far from a handy loo and if your job involves travelling make allowances for extra stops *en route* if necessary. However, do consult your doctor if you have pain or discomfort on passing urine.

If you sometimes feel faint in the early days try moving your weight from one foot to another. If you think you are going to faint, sit down (on the ground if necessary) and let your head drop between your knees. This may not be particularly elegant, but then neither is collapsing in a heap.

"The last placement I was on involved travelling three days a week by train and bus. I finally gave up when I was sick on the bus."
Amanda (30) trainee psychologist

EATING

Whether you have lunch in a staff canteen, get snacks from a supermarket or regularly sit down to expense-account meals, you and your baby need a healthy, balanced diet.

The simplest way to ensure you get this is to think of food in five main groups. The chart below lists the groups and gives a simple way to balance your intake from each one.

Group 1 bread, other cereals and potatoes	eat **lots**
Group 2 fruit and vegetables	eat **lots**
Group 3 milk and dairy foods	eat or drink **moderate amounts** and choose lower fat versions where possible
Group 4 meat, fish and alternatives	eat **moderate amounts** and choose **lower fat** meat where possible Oily fish such as sardines or mackerel may be beneficial for health
Group 5 fatty and sugary foods	eat **sparingly** – that's to say infrequently and/or in small amounts

You don't have to balance every meal this way so even if the kind of food available at work falls short of these guidelines, you can even things out by planning your breakfast and evening meal with healthy eating in mind. Try to aim for a healthy balance on a daily basis. You should certainly be able to achieve it over a week or so.

Choosing a wide variety of foods from the top four groups every day will not only give you and your baby all the nutrients you need, but will help keep you fit and healthy, less prone to heartburn or constipation, and less likely to put on so much weight that you find it hard to regain your figure after childbirth.

Healthy eating checklist

- Choose a wide variety of foods from the top four groups every day.
- Keep the suggested balance in mind when you plan meals or shop for food.
- Eat plenty of bread, cereals and potatoes – especially wholemeal, wholegrain and high fibre versions.
- Eat at least five portions of fruit and vegetables daily.
- Go for lower fat foods but check the nutrient information labels to compare fat content; don't be misled by labels that claim a product is 'low fat', as others may be lower. And don't confuse 'low fat' foods with 'low calorie' ones: low calorie foods often use sugar substitutes which some research suggests may be dangerous in excess.
- Trim fat from meat, remove skin from poultry and cook fish without batter.
- Cook where possible without added fat – try grilling, poaching, baking, steaming or boiling instead of roasting or frying.
- Try beans and pulses instead of meat as they are naturally low in fat.
- Use spreading fats and cooking oils sparingly.
- Only have cakes, biscuits, ice-cream, puddings, sweets, chocolate etc. as occasional treats. You don't need fatty and sugary foods for a healthy diet, but they give you extra choice and flavour.
- Look for snack substitutes: dried apricots instead of sweets or biscuits; a glass of fruit juice instead of cola; a breadstick in place of crisps.

Pregnancy is not the time to go on a slimming diet, but equally it isn't true that you need to eat for two. What you need are regular, balanced meals. So don't skip lunch altogether. And even if you feel too tired in the early days to do much cooking in the evenings, find ways of making sure you can eat well without going to too much trouble. A baked potato with cheese and a salad followed by fruit and a yoghurt is just as quick and easy as a fry-up with chips and a slice of Swiss roll – and much better for you.

If you have to follow a special diet for medical reasons, or if you are worried whether you are eating the right sort of food, ask your doctor if you can see a dietitian for further advice.

Foods to avoid when pregnant

You should try to avoid all types of pate and some ripened soft cheeses, such as Camembert, Brie and blue-veined cheese like Gorgonzola and Stilton because they may contain high levels of **listeria**, a bacterium that can cause listeriosis. This can result in miscarriage, stillbirth or severe illness in a newborn. 'Cook-chill' meals can also contain high levels of listeria, so you should always heat them until they are piping hot, never reheat them, and never eat them cold.

Raw and partly cooked eggs, poultry and raw meat can contain the **salmonella** bacterium that can cause salmonella food poisoning, so avoid any dishes containing uncooked eggs, and ensure that meat and eggs are always cooked thoroughly. Although salmonella may not have a direct effect on your unborn child it is sensible to avoid it.

Rare and raw meat may also be infected with an organism called **toxoplasma gondii**, as may unwashed vegetables and salads, and untreated goats' milk. This organism causes toxoplasmosis, which can result in a range of problems if passed to an unborn baby.

If you drink milk it is best to stick to pasteurised or UHT milk as untreated milk – usually sold in green-top bottles or cartons marked 'unpasteurised' – may contain a variety of potentially harmful organisms and should be avoided in pregnancy.

DRINKING

These days it is socially much more acceptable to turn down the offer of alcohol and ask for mineral water or fruit juice instead. So women whose jobs involve entertaining clients, or those who enjoy going to the pub or wine bar with their colleagues, are less likely to feel the odd woman out if they stick to soft drinks.

During pregnancy, alcohol that cannot be coped with by the liver flows into the mother's bloodstream and gets passed, via the placenta, to the growing baby. Any possible risks to your child are greatest during the very early weeks, so it is probably wiser not to drink at all during this time.

What about later on? For women who aren't pregnant the medically recommended sensible drinking guideline is not more than 14 units of alcohol spread through the week, with one or two drink-free days (a unit is explained below). During pregnancy the advice is to drink less than this or to give up alcohol altogether.

Studies have shown that even moderate drinking (more than 10 units a week) may be harmful to the foetus, being associated with congenital abnormalities, a higher incidence of stillbirths, growth retardation and delayed physical and mental development. Binge drinking (5 or 6 units on one occasion) is also harmful. Heavy alcohol consumption (more than 8 units a day) during pregnancy can result in a child being born with foetal alcohol syndrome, where the baby is born with facial and physical deformities, may be mentally retarded and slow to grow and develop.

The number of units in a drink will depend on its strength and its measure. Drinks poured at home, for example, tend to be more generous than those you buy in pubs or wine bars. As a rough guide the following would apply to pub measures:

- half a pint of ordinary strength beer, lager or cider (3.5% ABV*) = 1 unit
- one small glass of wine (8% ABV) = 1 unit
- one single measure of spirits (40% ABV) = 1 unit
- one small glass of sherry or port (20% ABV) = 1 unit

(*ABV means alcohol by volume and appears on most labels)

To sum up, the occasional social drink later on is unlikely to cause any harm providing you make sure your blood alcohol level stays low all the time. So don't binge, and if you do drink alcohol, sip your drink to make it last. Your liver can only process about one unit of alcohol per hour.

The dangers of drinking in pregnancy have been so well publicised that most people will accept this as a reason for avoiding alcohol. Even if you have not yet announced your pregnancy there are other socially acceptable excuses. You could say you are allergic to alcohol, or that you make it a rule not to drink during the working week. However, there are still people who think no one can relax and enjoy themselves unless they have a glass of something intoxicating in their hand. One way of dealing with this kind of bore is to agree to have one glass of wine and then keep it topped up with soda, or to get yourself a tonic with ice and lemon – who will know there is no gin or vodka in it?

There is no firm evidence to show that drinking tea or coffee has any adverse effect on your baby, but clearly it is sensible to avoid drinking anything in excess. Some women find they go off the taste anyway and prefer switching to fruit juice or water.

SMOKING

If you smoke, you should give up during pregnancy for your baby's sake as well as your own. Giving up is one of the best things you can do for your health and that of your child. Smoking during pregnancy affects the functioning of the placenta, reducing the supply of oxygen and nutrition to the developing foetus. This can affect the baby's growth and development. Smoking can lead to a low birthweight and a greater risk that the baby will die around the time of the birth. Research has shown that women who smoke 15 or more cigarettes a day during pregnancy have at least twice the risk of miscarriage, twice as many low birthweight babies (leading to significantly more stillbirths) and a one-third greater chance of their baby dying during the first month of life. Even smoking a few cigarettes is harmful.

After the baby is born, a smoky environment can increase the risk of cot death and chest infections, especially in the first year, so it's much better if you (and your partner) don't smoke.

The earlier you stop smoking the better, ideally when you are thinking about getting pregnant, but it's never too late. Giving up during the first 16 weeks of pregnancy will be a particular help in protecting your baby from slow growth and low birthweight, but your baby will benefit from your quitting even as late as the 30th week. If you have tried to stop smoking before and not succeeded, you can try again. There are around ten million ex-smokers in the UK today – not all of them succeeded in quitting first time, either. You can do it too.

Knowing that smoking can be harmful to your baby may provide enough motivation to quit. Being made to feel guilty about smoking, without being given any encouragement or support, may just leave you feeling helpless and bad about yourself for not having more willpower. So you need to want to stop smoking for yourself, as well as for other people.

One way to find the motivation you need is to count the benefits of giving up smoking:

- Your health will improve immediately;
- You will protect the health of people around you;
- You will set a good example to your own and other people's children;
- If you stop in the first three months of pregnancy you will reduce the risk of having a low birthweight baby;
- Quitting at any time during pregnancy will benefit you and the baby;
- You'll save money;
- You'll smell nicer;
- You'll feel more in control of your life and should get a sense of achievement in giving up.

Making plans to stop smoking a little while before you actually do so can increase your chances of success. You might think about the reasons why you smoke, the times you are most likely to feel like a cigarette, and the things that worry you about giving up. The nicotine in cigarettes is a highly addictive drug. When you smoke, blood levels of nicotine rise, but fall soon after, giving you a feeling of withdrawal. By smoking, you avoid those feelings of discomfort and this gives you the illusion that smoking has made you feel good.

Smoking can also become a habit. You may associate smoking with certain activities such as having a cup of coffee or talking on the phone. These habits build up over time, but being aware of the 'danger' times will help you avoid such situations or stiffen your resolve against reaching for a cigarette. Keeping a diary for a few days may help you pinpoint the times when you smoke, the reasons why, and the moods associated with your smoking. Being able to see patterns to your smoking will help you work out strategies for giving up.

Coping strategies

- Get your family and friends to support you. Ask them to understand if you feel irritable or down.
- You may find it helpful to avoid people who smoke – or to ask them not to smoke around you.
- When you feel the urge for a cigarette, do something else instead: have a (non-alcoholic) drink, chew some gum, pick up a magazine, do some exercise.
- Keep your hands occupied with something else: doodling, for example, or even worry beads!
- If you associate smoking with tea or coffee, switching to soft drinks might help.
- Plan some rewards for yourself. Save the money you would have spent on cigarettes and then use it for a treat.

Once you have worked out your own plan, set a date within the next two weeks so that you act while your motivation is still high. Decide to give up, choose a day, and go for it.

If you need some extra help your GP or antenatal clinic should have a copy of the free Health Education Authority booklet *Stopping Smoking Made Easier*. Or you could phone the Smokers' Quitline (see 'Addresses' on page 217) for details of local support services.

EXERCISE

If you are holding down a job, running a home and having a baby, you may feel you have neither the time nor the energy to fit in any form of exercise as well. Certainly, during both the early and late stages of pregnancy, you may be too tired to contemplate any additional exertion, but the middle months may be a different matter.

It is worth considering doing some exercise because it is important to keep fit during pregnancy and prepare yourself for labour. It is also a good idea to make some time for yourself each day when you can get in touch with the needs of your own body. Exercise can also help to alleviate stress. If you feel under pressure trying to balance the demands of work, home and pregnancy then taking some time out for regular exercise may give you more energy to cope with everything else in your life, rather than finishing you off altogether.

So what kind of exercise could you do?

- **Sports and keep-fit.** Providing you are in good health and have no previous history of miscarriage or premature labour, doctors agree that you can continue most sports or exercise routines. However, most also advise against sports that are especially vigorous or dangerous, such as horse-riding, ski-ing or marathon running. Whatever form of exercise you do, you should never go on until you feel exhausted and you should always stop if you feel any pain. If you are not sure whether you can exercise safely, or if you are expecting twins (or more), check with your doctor beforehand. If sport is not part of your life and you have no established exercise plan, this is not the time to take up anything particularly demanding – but this does not mean that all forms of physical activity must be ruled out.

- **Swimming.** Swimming is good all-round exercise, ideal in pregnancy when the illusion of weightlessness is wonderful. You can improve your fitness and become more supple, and even if you can't swim you can use the support of the water in a swimming pool to help you do some gentle water exercises. Try to find a pool that is fairly warm so that you lessen the risk of getting cramp.
- **Walking.** This is one form of exercise that requires very little outlay, apart from a comfortable pair of shoes.
- **Yoga and other exercise classes.** Some classes are specifically designed for pregnant women. Your local library or health centre may have details, or you could ask your local branch of the National Childbirth Trust.

Many of the books about pregnancy and childbirth also suggest exercises you can do at home. However, many women prefer to enrol in classes – partly because the commitment to a class means they are more likely to keep up an exercise programme and partly because the teacher will be able to make sure the exercises are being done correctly. Going to a class is also a good way of meeting other women who may later be part of the support network every working parent needs.

HOW WILL YOU FIT IN EXERCISE?

When you are considering the kind of exercise you might do, you need also to think realistically about fitting it in with everything else. It is no good booking for a yoga class that takes place in the evening, for instance, if the effort involved getting there after a long day at work is going to be so great that you are more than likely to give up after a week or so.

There may be a swimming pool near your home or workplace.

Does it have early morning sessions? Could you swim during the lunch-hour or after you finish for the day?

Walking can be done at any time. You can even make it part of your daily routine, by walking to the next bus stop instead of the one you usually wait at, for example.

HEALTH HAZARDS AT WORK

As well as making sure you are doing all you can to safeguard your health and that of your baby, you need to know that your working environment is safe.

New health and safety rules put a legal responsibility on employers to carry out risk assessments in respect of working conditions, processes and materials, to make sure they do not damage the health of a pregnant woman, a new mother or one who is still breastfeeding. If there is such a risk, the employer must take whatever preventative or protective action that is required by any specific legislation.

If a risk still remains, the employer must alter the woman's working conditions or hours of work – and if that is not reasonable, or still fails to avoid the risk, the employer has to offer the woman any suitable alternative work that is available. If this is not possible, an employer must suspend the woman from work on normal pay.

WORKING WITH CHEMICALS

It has long been established that specific jobs may present specific risks for pregnant women if those jobs involve exposure to specific substances. Women who work in the chemical and cleaning industries come into contact with powerful chemicals that should be avoided in pregnancy. Pesticides and insecticides can also be dangerous and certain chemicals used in dyeing, hairdressing and dry cleaning can also have side effects on the mother and the unborn child.

The list of these dangerous substances is long and still increasing; every year it is estimated that between 700 and 3000 new industrial chemicals are introduced and nobody knows with any certainty what effects they could have on the human reproductive system.

WHAT YOU CAN DO

- **Raise the issue with your employer. All products used in the workplace must be supplied with information regarding their safe use, so even if your employer is not initially sure whether something might be hazardous in pregnancy, it should be possible to find out.**
- **Your trade union rep, if you have one, may be able to give you information.**
- **You can phone the Employment Medical Advisory Service if you need confidential advice from a team of doctors and nurses. EMAS is run by the Health and Safety Executive and you can check your local phone book for the number of the nearest regional headquarters.**

BIOLOGICAL HAZARDS

Women working in microbiological laboratories tend to be protected by the regulations covering all staff. However, women working with animals – for example, in veterinary practices or on farms – may be more at risk because they may come unwittingly into contact with organisms which can be hazardous in pregnancy. Chlamydia, for example, is a bacterium that can be transmitted by sheep during lambing and can cause premature labour, miscarriage or stillbirth. It may also lead to eye infections and pneumonia in a newborn baby. Toxoplasmosis, which is caused by an organism called toxoplasma gondii, can be transmitted from the faeces of cats as well as via certain foods (see above) and can cause a range of foetal abnormalities.

However, the most likely biological hazard is the risk of German measles (rubella), which can affect an unborn baby if you catch it in the first four months of pregnancy. Women such as teachers or nursery staff who work with young children are particularly vulnerable.

WHAT YOU CAN DO

- **Get someone else to empty cat litter trays or wear disposable gloves if you have to do it. Trays should be cleaned every day and filled with boiling water for five minutes.**
- **Avoid contact with sick cats.**
- **Wear gloves for gardening in case the soil is contaminated with faeces.**
- **If you do come into contact with cat faeces, wash your hands thoroughly.**
- **If you work with young children, make sure you have been tested to see if you are immune to rubella (this is normally done routinely at your first antenatal visit). If you are not immune you will not be able to have a vaccination until after the birth. You may have to let people know you are pregnant as early as possible to enlist their co-operation in avoiding contact with cases of German measles.**
- **If you do come into contact with rubella, and you are not immune, tell your doctor at once. Blood tests at fortnightly intervals will show whether you have been infected and you will then be able to consider what action to take.**

- **Avoid lambing or milking ewes and all contact with newborn lambs**

X-RAYS, ULTRASOUND AND VDUS

X-rays may affect an unborn child and the Health and Safety Executive has laid down standards for women working in hospitals and other laboratories. X-ray machines are also widely used for security checks but there is probably little risk to anyone passing through the system.

Ultrasound is also used widely in industry, and expert opinion holds that the dosage used is probably safe.

At present, any link between VDUs and reproductive hazards is unproved. Since the beginning of the 1980s, when VDUs were first introduced on a large scale, there have been a few reports linking constant use with miscarriages and birth defects. However, a review of recent studies said that "at present it seems reasonable to conclude that pregnancy will not be harmed by using VDUs. Statements to the contrary are not soundly based."

While more research is being carried out, some countries allow pregnant women the right to move, if they choose, to other equivalent work not involving VDUs during their pregnancy, or to take leave during their pregnancy without loss of their employment rights.

WHAT YOU CAN DO

- **Your employer should be aware of the guidelines regarding the use of X-ray and ultrasound machines. If you need advice, contact EMAS (see above).**
- **If you use a VDU, make sure you are sitting comfortably and interrupt your work at the screen with regular breaks or changes of activity.**

- **If you are concerned about the possible risks, talk to your personnel officer or union rep about the possibility of transferring to other work, without the loss of pay, status or career prospects.**

PASSIVE SMOKING

The chemicals in cigarette smoke can cut the supply of oxygen and vital nutrients to your baby and slow down its growth. Most women know they should not smoke during pregnancy, and it is also advisable to avoid breathing in other people's smoke.

More and more companies already have workplace policies on smoking: Action on Smoking and Health (ASH) estimates that one UK company in five has a formal written smoking policy and up to 80 per cent of large firms have some sort of restrictions. In Autumn 1992, the Health and Safety Executive published new guidance notes for employers, warning that passive smoking at work can damage non-smokers' health. The implications for workplace smoking may be profound, with employers no longer able to ignore the issue, and more and more of them developing comprehensive no-smoking policies.

WHAT YOU CAN DO

- **Raise the issue of passive smoking with your employer. If your workplace does not have a policy about smoking at work, suggest one is introduced.**
- **Canvass the support of colleagues – others may welcome smoke-free zones.**
- **In the meantime, ask if you can move to work with non-smokers or ask the smokers if they would mind smoking elsewhere**
- **Send off for a copy of *Smoking At Work: An Employee's Guide***

to Clearing the Air, available free to people who have a problem about others smoking in the workplace, from ASH, the anti-smoking campaign.

LIFTING AND CARRYING

Many women worry if they have to lift or carry heavy things during pregnancy – although second-time-round mothers know that it is often impossible to avoid carrying a hefty toddler! Even so, the hormonal changes that take place when you are pregnant soften your ligaments so handling heavy loads can exacerbate back problems.

WHAT YOU CAN DO

- Draw your employers' attention to the problem. There are regulations that require employers to take steps to reduce the risk of manual handling injury and to be aware that allowance should be made for pregnancy.
- If you are lifting anything, bend your knees and use your leg muscles to straighten up rather than stooping over, which strains your back.

If you are worried about any aspect of your working environment, check it out with your doctor, employer or trade union official. If you still need advice or information, contact your regional office of the Health and Safety Executive and ask to speak to someone in the Employment Medical Advisory Service. You can find the number in your local phone book or from the head office in London.

ANTENATAL CARE AND CLASSES

YOUR RIGHTS

One of your rights when you are pregnant and working is to have paid time off for antenatal care. This includes all the appointments you will have to monitor your pregnancy. It can also include any classes in preparation for labour, birth and parenthood.

If your antenatal appointments fall within or near to your working hours, your employer must allow you time off to attend them, including the time you need to travel to the clinic, GP or hospital, without docking your pay. For your part, you should let your employer know when you need time off and how long you are likely to be away. After your first visit your employer can ask to see a certificate, signed by a doctor, midwife or health visitor, stating you are pregnant and a card showing that an appointment has been made. If your employer will not give you time off, or if your pay is stopped for the time you take – or if you are dismissed for asserting your rights to these things – you can make a claim to an Industrial Tribunal (see page 68). This has to be done within three months.

Where time off for antenatal care includes relaxation and parentcraft classes, your employer may ask to see a letter from your GP, midwife or health visitor, to say that these classes are part of your antenatal care.

WHY GO TO CLASSES?

It is important to attend antenatal classes, as well as your antenatal appointments, for a number of reasons. They will help you prepare mentally and physically for childbirth. If you know what is happening you will be able to work with your body instead of against it and are more likely to find the birth a satisfying experience.

If you hope to give birth in a particular way – naturally, without the use of drugs, for example – you are more likely to get what you want if you know the reasons why you are asking for things. Classes can help you sort out in your own mind the things that are most important to you and give you the confidence to ask for them. Classes can also help reassure you if you have any anxieties about the process of childbirth.

Antenatal classes may be run at your GP's surgery, elsewhere in the community such as a local hall, or at the hospital where you are booked in for the birth. Your midwife will be able to give you information about when and where these are held. If you are having your baby in hospital, a tour of the labour and delivery rooms is generally arranged so that you can familiarise yourself with the hospital and some of the staff.

"It was nice to see some familiar faces when I was in labour and the physiotherapist who talked to us about relaxation techniques also turned up on the ward after I'd had the baby, to talk about postnatal exercises."

Irene (32) teacher

In the past classes used to be timetabled so that women went towards the end of their pregnancy, simply because most women would have stopped working by this time. Now that more women work for longer in their pregnancies this is not always the case. In some places two separate sets of classes are on offer, the first, held in the early months, concentrates on pregnancy, the second on labour, delivery and coping with a newborn. The people who give the classes may well be some of those you will meet later on.

The National Childbirth Trust also runs classes in preparation for childbirth. You have to pay for these; fees vary between £25 and £80 for a set of eight classes, plus a reunion after all the babies have arrived. Classes are held in the evenings as well as during the day. Some are for women only, others for couples. Even if this is not your first child, going to 'refresher' classes can be useful.

"Going to the NCT classes with my partner helped us feel very close – we were able to share everything including the birth. It made it our baby right from the start."

Paul (34) teacher

Another good reason for attending antenatal classes is that they give you a good opportunity to meet other women having babies around the same time as yourself. When you are working, particularly if you are working late into your pregnancy, it can be hard to share your enthusiasm or excitement about the baby with colleagues who have not yet had children or whose offspring are well past the baby stage. Other pregnant women form a kind of sisterhood. They will sympathise with and encourage your need to focus on the baby as well as other parts of your life.

"The first time I met another pregnant woman was at my first antenatal class. It was such a relief after seven months to discover that I wasn't going completely mad, alone!"

Kate (33) lecturer in stage management

The friendships that form in this way can not only play an important supporting role during pregnancy, but can gel into a network of support after the baby is born. New parents need all the support they can get, and for those who are going back to work this is particularly important. Knowing people who have children of the same age can help you share the load; you can babysit for each other when the children are younger, you can share the school run when the children are older. You can swap information about local facilities – after school clubs, holiday playschemes. Building up such a network is crucial if you are a working parent – and it is never too soon to start.

"The people at work were very nice and asked all the right questions – did I want a boy or girl, was the baby moving yet? But I couldn't really talk to them in the same way as I could to the other women in my class. Just about everything came up, from how hard it was to make love with a bump to whether we were worried about having stitches.

I'd worked for the lab for six years and made some good friends. But in the eight weeks I went to classes I got closer to some of the women than I had been to anyone since I made friends at school."

Elaine (31) lab technician

4 YOUR RIGHTS AT WORK

Women working in pregnancy have specific rights in law and you will be entitled to all or some of them. Occasionally employers take the trouble to explain your maternity rights once they have formally been told of your pregnancy; others may not fully understand the law or may leave it to you to find out what the correct procedures are.

The Department of Employment produces a booklet called *Maternity Rights*, which was designed to be user-friendly. Although it is comprehensive it is still quite complicated to follow. A shorter, simpler leaflet, *Pregnant at Work Update*, is available from the Maternity Alliance.

The rights that are explained in these publications – and summarised below – are all laid down by law. However, some women work for organisations or companies that offer better deals than the legal minimum. You can find out if this applies to you by checking with your employer, either directly or through the personnel department, or asking your union representative.

PAID TIME OFF FOR ANTENATAL CARE

All pregnant women, no matter how long they have been working for a particular company nor how many hours they work, are entitled to **time off for antenatal care**, including the time needed to travel to the clinic or the GP. They are also entitled to be paid for this time at their normal rate of pay. You should let our employer know when you need time off and how long you are likely to be away.

After the first appointment an employer is entitled to ask to see a certificate confirming the pregnancy, signed by a doctor, mid-wife or health visitor, and an appointment card or other document showing that an appointment has been made.

MATERNITY LEAVE

All women who are in work when they are pregnant are entitled to **14 weeks' maternity leave**.

New legislation came into effect in 1994 that meant that even part-timers and women who had only just started a job were entitled to maternity leave. Now all women, regardless of the hours they work or the length of time they have been in a particular job, are entitled to 14 weeks' maternity leave.

During this time, all your contractual rights – things like pension rights, holiday entitlement, your company car – remain yours just as they would if you had been at work. However, instead of getting your usual wages you will receive either Statutory Maternity Pay or Maternity Allowance (see below). At the end of your leave you are entitled to go back to the same job. Some employers offer **adoption leave** on the same terms as maternity leave. This is not, however, a statutory duty.

To get maternity leave:

- Write to your employers at least 21 days before you start your maternity leave, saying you are pregnant and giving them the date of the week you expect to have the baby (your GP or hospital will tell you the expected date of delivery – the EDD);

- Tell your employer the date you intend to start your maternity leave: this need only be in writing if your employer asks for it;
- If your employer asks for it, also enclose a copy of the maternity certificate (form MAT B1) which your midwife or GP will give you when you are about six months pregnant;
- If you can't give 21 days' notice (if you are suddenly taken into hospital, for example) then you must write to your employers as soon as you reasonably can.

The earliest you can start maternity leave is 11 weeks before the week in which the baby is due – but it is up to you to decide when you want to stop. You can, if you feel up to it, work right up until the week of childbirth. The one exception to this rule is if, during the last six weeks, you are off work for some reason connected with your pregnancy. Under those circumstances your employer could decide to start you on your maternity leave, even if you are absent for only one day.

GOING BACK TO WORK

Your employer may provide a better maternity deal than the statutory minimum. If this is the case, you need to check the details. However, the following applies to women who are only entitled to the legal minimum.

- You don't have to give any notice of your return if you are going back at the end of the 14-week period; you can just turn up at work on the first day of the following week.

    The date you are due back at work will depend on when you started your leave. If you left at the earliest possible opportunity – 11 weeks before your baby was due – you will be due back when your baby is a few weeks old (the exact age will depend on when the baby actually arrived). If you worked as late as possible, you will have more time with your baby before you have to make up your mind.

- If you want to go back earlier, you must give your employers seven days' notice in writing. If you don't follow the rules, they can send you home again for seven days or until the end of the 14 weeks, whichever comes first.
- If you want to delay your return to work, there are three possibilities:
  - No matter when you started your leave, you are entitled to a minimum of two weeks at home after the birth. This may apply if you started your leave early and your baby arrives late.
  - If you are ill at the end of your 14 weeks and therefore can't return to work, you should be able to get sick pay from your employers
  - it may be possible to use the sex discrimination laws to establish that you have a right to more leave than the minimum 14 weeks. If you are unhappy about the prospect of returning to work so soon, talk things over with your trade union rep or seek independent advice from an organisation like the Maternity Alliance or the Citizens' Advice Bureau or a law centre.
- If you decide not to return to work, you should resign in the normal way. For example, if your contract stipulates that your normal notice period is one week, you need to inform your employer a week before the date you are due to return to work that you are resigning.

MATERNITY ABSENCE

Some women qualify for a longer period anyway: they are the ones entitled to **maternity absence**. Remember, all women qualify for 14 weeks maternity leave. But if you have either worked two years full-time (16 hours or more a week) or five years part-time (8–16 hours a week) for the same employer, you will also be entitled to **29 weeks** off, from the week of the baby's birth. This may overlap with the 14 weeks maternity leave, which is, unfortunately rather confusing.

To apply for this longer period of leave you simply follow the same steps as you would if you were applying for the 14 weeks leave (see above), with one important addition. When you write to your employer you must state that it is your intention to return to work after the birth.

It is worth noting that the qualifying period extends up to the end of the twelfth week before the baby is due. So even if you have not clocked up enough years to qualify at the beginning of your pregnancy, you my have done so by the time you need to apply for leave.

Unfortunately, women who work in a firm which employs five people or less do not have a clear right to return after 29 weeks, even if they have worked these hours, although they still qualify for the 14-weeks leave (see above).

GOING BACK TO WORK AFTER MATERNITY ABSENCE

- You **may** get a letter from your employers any time from 11 weeks after the start of your maternity leave, asking you to confirm in writing that you are going back to work. If you stopped work as soon as possible (11 weeks before your baby was due), this letter could arrive at around the same time as your baby. You may feel unable to think straight at this point, you may even be having second thoughts about returning, but if you want to keep your options open, you **must** write and say you do. **If you don't reply within 14 days you will lose your right to return**.

You probably won't have to say **when** you intend to go back, if the letter does arrive at this stage, especially if you are planning to take the full entitlement of 29 weeks' leave after the birth.

- However, the latest you can make your mind up is around four weeks before the end of this 29-week part of the leave as you must give your employer at least three weeks' written notice of the day on which you want to start work again. Even so, this should give you some time to see how you feel and how things are working out.

  Your child will be six months old at this point – and the difference between a newborn and a six-month-old baby is enormous. More to the point, your feelings about whether you want to be a full-time mother or not may have changed by this time too.

- If you want to go back to work earlier, before the 29 weeks are up, you can do so, providing you give your employer at least three weeks' written notice of the date you intend to return.

- If you want to delay your return you can do so
  - if you are ill, providing you let your employers know before the day you were due back that you are extending your leave because of sickness. You must also send them a medical certificate.
  - if you are prevented from going back to work by, for example, a strike.

  On the other hand, your employers can ask you to post-pone you date of return for up to four weeks, provided they can give you specific reasons and a new start-by date.

- If you tell your employers you are going back to work and then change your mind, even at the last minute, there is nothing they can do about it. Under most circumstances you can even keep your SMP. If, however, you were given a contract or a policy document which contained a clause about repaying any amount over and above the basic rate if you failed to return, seek advice from a trade union representative, a law centre or the Citizens' Advice Bureau.

Working out when to stop work and when to start again is not always straightforward. (There is more information in Chapter 6 on going back to work.) Will you really want 11 weeks at home before the birth or would you rather work as long as possible on full pay? Knowing what you are entitled to in terms of cash may help you decide.

PAY DURING MATERNITY LEAVE

STATUTORY MATERNITY PAY (SMP)

You will be able to claim SMP if you meet certain qualifications. First, you must have worked for the same employer for at least 26 weeks ending with the qualifying week. This is the 15th week before the week the baby is due.

If you are in any doubt, check the calendar and find the Sunday before your EDD (Estimated Date of Delivery). If the baby is due on a Sunday, that is the date you start from. Now count back 15 Sundays. If you have worked for your employer for at least 26 weeks by the end of that week, you meet the first requirement.

Second, you must still be employed In your job in that 15th week. (Being off sick or on holiday does not matter.)

Third, you must earn more on average than the lower earnings limit for National Insurance contributions, currently £57 per week. It is important to know that if you are off sick around the middle of your pregnancy and your earnings are badly affected, this may affect your rights to SMP or the amount you will get.

You can get SMP even if you are not planning to return to work after having your baby. If you intend to return and then change your mind, you won't have to pay it back.

If you are not sure whether you are entitled to SMP or not, ask for it anyway. Your employer will work out whether or not you should get it.

SMP is paid for up to 18 weeks. It can be paid from the 11th week before the birth (the earliest time at which you can start maternity leave) but it is not paid for any week you work. So if you qualify for only 14 weeks' maternity leave and you return to work after this, you won't get the remaining four weeks' SMP. On the other hand, you no longer lose any SMP if you work later into your pregnancy, even right up to the time your baby is due – if you then qualify for maternity absence as well as maternity leave you will get the full 18 weeks' SMP.

For the first six weeks SMP is paid at the rate of 90 per cent of your average pay. After that you get the basic rate of £52.50 per week. To claim it, write to your employers to ask for it at least three weeks before you stop work. Send them a copy of the maternity certificate (MAT B1). Your employers will probably pay you the same way you are usually paid your wages, either weekly or monthly, and they will deduct any tax and National Insurance contributions.

Normally you decide when you want to stop work and start getting SMP. But if you are off work during the last six weeks of your pregnancy, due to a pregnancy-related illness, you won't be able to claim statutory sick pay (SSP), but will start getting maternity pay instead. If your illness has nothing to do with your pregnancy, you can claim SSP until you start maternity leave and pay.

MATERNITY ALLOWANCE

If you don't qualify for SMP, you may still be able to claim maternity allowance. This may apply to you if you are self-employed or if you gave up work or changed jobs during your pregnancy. To qualify you have to have paid National Insurance (NI) contributions for at least 26 of the 66 weeks before the week the baby is due.

To claim you need form MA1 from your antenatal clinic or social security office. Fill this in and send it with your maternity certificate MAT B1, to your social security office as soon as you can once you are 26 weeks pregnant. If you are still waiting for your maternity certificate, don't delay – you can send it on later.

If you have not paid 26 weeks NI contributions by the time you reach the 26th week of pregnancy you can carry on working and send off the MA1 form as soon as you have made the magic 26 NI payments. If you are not sure whether you are entitled to maternity allowance, claim anyway. Your social security office will be able to work out whether you should get it or not.

Maternity allowance is paid for up to 18 weeks any time from 11 weeks before the week your baby is due. It is only paid for weeks when you are not working and is usually paid by order book that can be cashed at your nearest post office. There are two rates: £52.50 a week if you were employed, or £44.55 a week if you were self-employed or not employed in the qualifying week (i.e. the 15th week before the week your baby is due).

PROTECTION AGAINST DISMISSAL

Since 16 October 1994 it has been unlawful to dismiss any woman, regardless of her length of service, or single her out for redundancy over other similarly employed people, because she is pregnant or taking maternity leave.

If you are dismissed or made redundant you are entitled to be given written reasons. If you think the reason is connected to your pregnancy, take advice from your union, Citizens' Advice Bureau or solicitor as you may have grounds to complain of unfair dismissal at an industrial tribunal.

You may also be able to make a claim under the sex discrimination laws if you lose your job or have your conditions of work changed because you are pregnant or have a baby. The law is complicated in these areas, though, so you will need to take advice. Consult your union if you have one, the Citizens' Advice Bureau, a local law centre, the Maternity Alliance or The Equal Opportunities Commission.

If you are going to complain to an industrial tribunal your complaint must normally be made within three months of the date when the infringement of your right occurred. To start the process off you will need form IT1 (or IT(Scot) if you live in Scotland) and the accompanying leaflet ITL1. You can get these from the local office of the Employment Service.

PATERNITY LEAVE

Although the majority of working fathers take some time off when a child is born, employers are not legally obliged to give paternity leave. Some, however, do allow men paid time off, on or near the time of the birth. The length of leave may be just a few days or longer. Sometimes there is a service or seniority requirement. If an employer does not offer paternity leave, fathers have to use their holiday entitlement or arrange to take unpaid leave.

BETTER THAN BASIC?

It is always worth finding out whether your employer offers more than the basic maternity pay and rights package, to make sure that you get everything you are entitled to. You might also consider negotiating with your employer, to see if you can get a better deal.

There are several ways in which employers can offer their staff more than they are legally obliged to. They may allow women a longer period of maternity leave, or while they are on leave they may pay them at a higher rate or for a longer time. Sometimes the improved package is only on offer to those who have been employed for a certain length of time or have reached a certain level of seniority. Sometimes the more generous offer is linked to conditions about returning to work, although if you accepted the deal and then changed your mind about returning, an employer might find it difficult to enforce this contract.

There are some organisations where women are offered a retraining programme when they return to work. Again, this tends to apply only if they have been with the company for a specified length of time and have certain skills or management potential.

Others, such as local authorities, may offer career breaks to all their staff. At the end of the break staff are offered work at the same level at which they left. During a recognised career break you might be required to work for a few weeks each year and attend the occasional one-day seminar. Your employer might also keep you in touch with developments at work and in your field by sending you reports and journals, as well as information about the organisation itself.

There is usually a limit to the time you can take off. However, some employers run 'reservist' schemes whereby they are under no obligation to rehire you, but they will put you on a reserve list and consider you for re-employment when a suitable vacancy comes up. The break for these schemes can usually be longer but there is less likely to be contact during the break.

"My baby was born prematurely at 27 weeks and my employers knew very little about benefits and entitlements. I had to do all the ground work myself and then check my wages meticulously to make sure everything was in order – all at a time when I was trying to cope with the possibility of my baby not surviving and the after-effects of a Caesarean!"

Yuri (27) customer accounts clerk

The information given here was right at the time of going to press, but the rules and regulations do change from time to time. In addition, the legislation is not always easy to understand – even employers can be muddled. So it is always a good idea to check with your trade union, Citizens' Advice Bureau, local law centre or the Maternity Alliance.

5 MATERNITY LEAVE

BEFORE THE BABY ARRIVES

ADJUSTING TO NOT WORKING

It may feel strange not having to get up and go to work in the morning. Although most women welcome the start of maternity leave, there may be other things they find they miss.

You may miss the structure of the working day, the challenge and stimulation, and the social life that may have revolved around your job. Even if you have friends outside work, you may miss contact with other adults or the sense of being part of an outside world.

People often define themselves by the job they do, consciously or unconsciously. It may feel strange to think of yourself in a different way, or to feel you've no longer got a clear role or identity.

Your job may always have come first. You may even have delayed the start of your maternity leave in order to work as long as possible. Now you are at home you may be worried about turning into a different, less business-like, you. However much you wanted the baby, going on maternity leave may be the point at which it dawns on you that life is going to be very different from now on. Colleagues may make even matters worse by telling you how lucky you are to be able to stay at home for a while.

These feelings are common. If you know someone who has been in the same position herself, it may help to share your uncertainties with her.

If you are worried about domesticity submerging the 'working' you, let your bosses or workmates know that you want to be kept in touch with what is going on at work. Ask them to send you newsletters, company magazines and anything else you would have had if you were working.

One survey by the Maternity Alliance found that almost one in three women (31 per cent) were asked to do some work while they were on maternity leave. Women have a right to refuse requests like this, but you might like to let people at work know you would be interested in being asked in the first place.

"I stopped at 29 weeks. My job was very tiring and I hadn't had a holiday for ages. I was looking forward to having some time to myself but I did miss my friends at work."

Virginia (34) housing officer

"I only had four weeks off before the baby was born. Ideally, I would have stopped earlier but it was a busy time of year for us and my family had already given us so much for the baby that there wasn't much left for me to do as far as shopping for nursery equipment or baby clothes. But once I stopped work it was nice to wake up and know I had the whole day ahead with only myself to think about."

Shireen (27) travel agent

"I stopped work four weeks before my baby was born. I was very tired by that stage and it was nice to relax, sit and sunbathe. By that time I was finding it hard to concentrate at work anyway, so I was glad not to have to make the effort any more."

Mandy (31) sales and administration

BEFORE THE BIRTH

Depending on how much time you are taking off before your baby's expected birthday, you may feel there is either too much or too little to do. Draw up a list of things that have to be done, and things that would simply be nice to do. If you have a partner, enjoy the time you have together before life changes for good. Many mothers add that it is important not to feel guilty about doing nothing – it may be your last chance for years!

The Pregnancy Book, which is given free to all first-time mothers, usually by their GP or antenatal clinic, has useful lists of essential items to help women decide what to get ready for the birth and what they will need for a new baby. Resist the temptation to buy too much, too soon. You'll get a much better idea of what is really essential once you and your baby get to know each other. Shopping may seem one way to stave off boredom, if you are bored at home, but it could prove to be an unnecessarily extravagant activity. Bear in mind, too, that you may be able to borrow some of the things you will eventually need, or get them second-hand. (Always check that equipment is safe. Your health visitor will help you decide if you are not sure.)

Depending on when your maternity leave starts you may already have been to antenatal classes, or you may be about to start going. Either way, now is probably a good time to brush up on what you need to know about labour and birth. Once again, *The Pregnancy Book* has a section on this and you will also be able to find other books on childbirth in your local library or bookshop.

Getting out and about during the day helps to avoid boredom and isolation, and can also be a way of making new friends and acquaintances who can provide the social contact you used to get at work. At the supermarket or the library, for example, you are more likely to meet neighbours who don't work, or who work part-time.

Even so, it may be difficult to find new friends. One way could be to join a local National Childbirth Trust (NCT) branch, even if you are not taking NCT classes. Local branches hold all kinds of events, ranging from talks to purely social occasions. The local library should have details of your nearest branch, or phone the NCT head office in London for more information.

If, on the other hand, you want to get away from babies and children, you could join the National Women's Register, which is an organisation originally set up 35 years ago for women who were at home with children, but who wanted to keep their minds active and lively. These days membership is open to all women, whether they go out to work or stay at home. Local groups organise their own programme of meetings, usually fortnightly in each other's homes. The content tends to reflect the interests of the people in the group. Topics may range from first aid to meditation. There may be discussions about books, films, and TV programmes. There may be speakers on assertion or how to make a hanging basket. Again, the local library should have information on local branches, or you can contact the national office in Norwich.

If you find yourself with a lot of spare time on your hands, think of things you would like to do which may be impossible once you have a baby to look after. Once the baby arrives it will be much more difficult to go out. It will be harder for you to give anyone – your partner, your friends, other children – your undivided attention. And it could be months before you have an unbroken night's sleep.

Is there a book you have wanted to read for a long time, a pile of magazines you have been waiting to dip in to, or a video you have been wanting to see? If you have a partner, would you like to get away for a weekend, just the two of you? If that's not possible, perhaps you'd like to go out for a meal or have some friends over for Sunday brunch. Is there something you'd like to do with an older child that won't be so easy with a baby in tow – a first visit to the cinema, for example.

> **Checklist**
>
> - Are my things ready for the birth?
> - Are things ready for the baby: clothes; equipment for sleeping/ transport / feeding; nappies?
> - Read up/go to classes on labour and birth
> - Make local friends and start to set up networks
> - Take gentle exercise: walk/swim/yoga
> - Treat yourself: do something enjoyable which there was no time for before

PATERNITY LEAVE

If your partner is expecting a baby, now is the time to make your final plans about how much time, if any, you will be able to take off when the baby arrives.

Employers have no legal obligation to give their staff paternity leave, although some do. This tends to be between two and ten days, taken on or near the time of birth, and you may have to have worked for the organisation for a specified length of time in order to qualify.

The TUC/Maternity Alliance guidelines on how to negotiate best practice suggest that all fathers should be entitled to at least ten days fully paid paternity leave to be taken around the time of the expected date of childbirth, with an option of unpaid leave for a longer period, provided that proper notification is given.

If you are not entitled to paternity leave and cannot negotiate a deal, you may have to take some of your holiday entitlement or ask for unpaid leave.

Most people agree that it is important for fathers to spend some time at home when babies are born. Not only can they help give their partner the support she needs, but they can begin to build a relationship with their child.

"I took two weeks off. I was entitled to one week's leave as part of the deal negotiated by my union and I took an extra week as holiday. I wanted to be there to support my girlfriend and to be with our baby. The baby was very sweet and I wouldn't have missed it for the world."

Mick (33) graphic artist

"At first I was a bit scared to pick the baby up – he seemed so small and fragile. But by the end of the week I was changing nappies like a veteran and I used to swing him to sleep in the Moses basket, which my wife couldn't do because her arms got tired. I wish I could have taken more time off, but it was a start. It made me feel special, like a proper father."

Ian (29) mechanic

EARLY DAYS WITH YOUR BABY

Having a baby of your own can be one of life's most wonderful experiences, arousing deep feelings of love, happiness and pride. Even so, it is important to recognise that other equally strong feelings may alternate with the good ones.

For a start, being at home with a baby is a complete contrast to being at work. The day is no longer split up into separate, manageable sections the way it used to be. Many mothers find that time seems to blur, nothing ever seems to get finished. Babies tend not to eat or sleep at predictable times. There may be days when you wonder whether life will ever get back to normal again.

If you are have been used to organising your time efficiently and planning your days, the contrast may be difficult to adjust to.

If you have always been efficient and competent at work it can be hard to feel a complete novice again. Even if this is not your first baby, you will probably discover that not all your tried and tested methods work on this child.

Your feelings are likely to be exacerbated by sheer exhaustion. Many women admit that although they got tired during pregnancy, they didn't know what tiredness was until after the baby was born. If the birth itself was difficult, or did not go the way you hoped or planned, you may still be in the recovery phase. Physically you may be healing after a Caesarean or an episiotomy. Emotionally you may still be sad or angry at what happened.

Even if things went well, your body probably looks and feels different from the way it did before you were pregnant. You may look at the outfits you used to wear to work and wonder if you will ever be able to wear them again.

If this is your first baby you will have no on-the-job experience of mothering. Anything and everything can be a source of concern. Why is the baby crying? Are you feeding properly? Although books can offer general advice, your particular model didn't arrive with its own instruction manual. You only learn what works best by trial and error.

By and large, being a parent is something you learn as you go along – so it's important to accept that its perfectly normal to muddle through at first and that there's no such thing as a perfect mother.

Other people may be full of suggestions, of course. And in the early days you are likely to have a lot of visitors. This, in itself, can be an additional strain.

HOW CAN YOU HELP YOURSELF?

- **Limit the initial number of visitors.** It is hard to say 'no' to people who tell you they are dying to see the baby but you could put them off by inviting them to a special celebration on a particular day instead.
- **When visitors do drop in, don't feel you have to wait on them hand and foot.** And if anyone asks if they can do anything, don't waste the opportunity. There must be something you need, whether it is a pan of potatoes peeled for supper or just someone to hold the baby while you take half an hour to wash and dry your hair.
- **Eat properly.** You may not have time to prepare and cook 'proper' meals but easy, fast food can be just as nourishing and healthy. A poached egg on wholemeal toast with a sliced tomato is as quick to prepare as a burger and chips.
- **Don't diet, especially if you are breastfeeding.** If you are worried about the fact that you haven't lost the weight you put on in pregnancy, make changes to what you eat. Cut down on fatty foods and fill up with bread, rice or pasta instead. Make sure you have plenty of fresh fruit and vegetables.
- **Breastfeeding can make you thirsty.** Avoid sugary drinks with 'empty calories' but keep plenty of water, milk or juice to hand.
- **Relax – sleep if you can – when the baby sleeps.** Don't use the time to rush around doing chores.
- **Get some exercise.** It may seem silly if you are feeling tired, but exercise will help you tone up again and can help relieve stress. Go swimming or for a walk in the fresh air. Ask your health visitor or your NCT group about postnatal exercise or yoga classes.
- **Find your own ways of dealing with stress.** If you have a partner, ask him to give you a massage. Get a relaxation tape out of the library or try the exercise on page 209.

- **Is there someone who could mind the baby for a little while,** to give you some time for yourself – perhaps to soak in the bath, or listen to music, or watch a favourite video?
- **Use the support groups there to help you.** Whether you are recovering from a Caesarean, worried about breastfeeding, being driven up the wall by a baby who won't stop crying, there will be someone you can call. For a list of helpful organisations see page 216.

"I felt as if I'd lost control of my life. At work I was used to making decisions and following them through. I knew what I was doing. But when I was at home with the baby I felt I was just muddling through. And at the end of the day I'd wonder where the time had gone. Nothing seemed to have got done at all."

Annie (28) merchandiser

"It was great not to have to meet other people's targets or live up to their expectations. I was learning how to be a mum, and my baby was teaching me. It was just lovely to be with her all day."

Jane (34) tele-sales supervisor

"I'm not surprised sleep deprivation is used as a form of torture."

Elly (24) proofreader

"I was like a zombie for the first three months. People kept ringing up and saying they'd got a little present for the baby. I found it hard to say they couldn't come round. But I remember times when I was in tears at the end of the day because it was simply too exhausting. I couldn't wait for everyone to leave us alone."

Sarah (35) picture researcher

PARTNERS

New mothers need mothering, too, and your partner, if you have one, is probably the first person you will turn to for support.

However, new fathers may also be feeling needy or uncertain. A man may, for example, feel that a baby is taking up too much of his partner's time and attention – and he may even feel guilty that he's feeling that way!

A first-time father will undoubtedly have underestimated the difference one small baby makes. There are nappies in the bathroom, a buggy in the hallway, muslin squares on the sofa. It is no longer possible to make plans without taking the baby into consideration. Activities have to be planned like military operations, taking into account feeding and sleeping times (the baby's, not his) and backed up with what seems an inordinate amount of equipment.

Above all, he may be keen for things to 'get back to normal', especially in the sexual side of the relationship. Yet many women are not only too tired for love-making, they lose all sexual desire for a while after having a baby.

Sometimes, too, expectations change. When people become parents they often unconsciously revert to the ways their own parents behaved, because this is the only pattern of family behaviour they know.

What can you both do?

- Try to understand that this may be a difficult time for both of you. See if you can sit down and talk about the feelings you *both* have.
- Renegotiate the division of household responsibilities to include childcare. Things don't have to be equal, so long as they feel balanced.
- As a mother, make sure you are not shutting your partner out. He needs to get to know the baby too. Encourage him to share the care, but try not to watch him with an eagle eye if he does

so. There is more than one way of changing a nappy or bathing a baby safely. It doesn't have to be your way.

- As a father, try not to leave the everyday care to your partner. The more you do for and with your baby, the closer you will get.

- Wait until you *both* feel ready before resuming sex – but make sure you don't avoid all physical contact in the meantime. Everyone needs cuddles.

- Take love-making slowly at first. You may need to try different positions to avoid rubbing scar tissue and you may need to use a lubricant.

"I was horrified when my husband asked me if I'd iron some shirts. I was getting up to feed in the night and I was dead on my feet. Before I had the baby we split all the household chores and did our own ironing, but because I was at home for six months he assumed things had changed. I pointed out that I was on maternity leave to care for the baby, not provide laundry services for him."

Linda (33) computer operator

"It was important for me to be at home after the birth, not just to help my partner but to get to know the baby. You can't get that kind of bonding if you're coming in at six or seven at night. It's crucial to be involved in everything whether it's changing nappies or rocking the baby to sleep. It's very rewarding, too."

Bryan (32) salesperson

FEELING LONELY

The days after the birth are usually busy. Your partner may be able to take some time off or members of your family may come to help. You probably get flowers or cards from your colleagues and work.

After the initial excitement and attention from well-wishers, you will probably find yourself left on your own – apart from the baby, of course. If work has been a big part of your life, both professionally and socially, you may begin to feel very lonely and isolated.

"There were days when I kissed my husband goodbye in the morning and never spoke to another adult again until he came back at night. I loved the baby, but I really missed adult company and there were days I felt like climbing the walls. I saw going back to work like the light at the end of a tunnel."

Elaine (42) lecturer

"I rang the office once or twice, but my colleagues weren't really interested in the baby and I sensed they didn't really know what to talk to me about. I wanted to know what was happening, but they just said 'nothing much.' In the end I stopped calling. It just made me more fed up."

Yuri (26) personal finance

One of the problems is that working women may know few people living nearby. They leave home in the morning, come back at night, and their friends are not necessarily locally based. Pre-baby this doesn't matter. But once you have a baby in tow it isn't always easy to keep in touch.

"We did try going out in the evenings to see friends, taking the baby along in a carrycot. But he always woke up and then refused to settle, so in the end it seemed more trouble than it was worth. We became virtual recluses until I felt happy leaving him with a babysitter when he was about six months old."

Samantha (27) journalist

One solution may be for a partner to adjust his work pattern for a while, perhaps getting home earlier or going to work later. He might be able to bring work home, to cut his hours that way.

Some men decide to take only a couple of days off around the time of the birth and delay taking any further leave or holiday entitlement until a little later on. They feel their help and support will be even more important then than in the very early days when friends and relatives are more likely to be around.

Building support networks

Whether you are blissfully happy on your own with your baby, or whether you feel beleaguered and alone, you need to build up a network of support that will stand you in good stead both now and in the future when you go back to work.

- **Your health visitor.** Of all the professionals you will meet during pregnancy and afterwards, the health visitor is the one who is there to help the whole family – and that includes you. She usually visits you at home to introduce herself when your baby is between ten and 14 days old. Not only will she be able to deal with any particular concerns you have regarding your child, but she can fill you in on the kinds of services that are available in your area. Because of her local knowledge she can be a valuable source of information about a wide range of things – so use her.
- **Neighbours.** Once you are at home all day you are more likely to get to notice others in the neighbourhood who do not go off to work each morning. They may be older people who have now retired or people who are not in paid, full-time work at the moment. They may be students or people working from home.

   Babies have a way of breaking the ice, so if you get a chance to get to know your neighbours, take it. The couple down the road may have grandchildren of their own, whom they rarely see. They might enjoy the chance to babysit for you once they know you, and your baby, better.

The woman opposite may have teenage children, and she may be years older than you. But she might welcome a chat and a cup of coffee one morning, and there is no age barrier to friendship. Even the teenagers might enjoy taking the baby out for a walk in the buggy once in a while.

Even if you don't need that kind of help now, it is worth building up the contacts for the future.

- **Special groups.** If you have made friends with other women who attended the same antenatal classes as yourself it is definitely worth keeping in touch as they will have babies of about the same age and will understand and share the experiences you are going through.

  You can also join groups set up for mothers with young children. Local branches of the National Childbirth Trust often arrange meetings and activities. Information about other mother and baby groups can usually be found in the local library, or by asking your health visitor.

  You can make friends, too, by going along to mother and baby swimming sessions at a local swimming pool.

  Parents at Work (formerly the Working Mothers Association) not only runs an information helpline but can put members in touch with a network of self-help groups run by and for working parents. Once you have paid your annual membership fee, you are sent an information pack, given unlimited access to the helpline and a contact name for the nearest local group. The main advantage of joining a group like this is that you already have something in common besides a baby – work. You can swap information about local childcare; you even have a chance to improve local provision by acting collectively. You may also be able to exchange valuable tips on any work-related problems.

  If you are on your own, you might also consider joining Gingerbread, another organisation with a network of local groups. Gingerbread provides information and advice as well as helping lone parents make friends. It can also offer the opportunity to develop new personal and professional skills.

Sometimes, though, it can feel difficult to break into an established group. Women who happily talked to anyone when they were at work often find their confidence evaporates once they have had a baby. They see women together at the clinic, but don't like to join in. They go along to a mother and baby morning at the church hall, but sit there for two hours not speaking to a soul. Most of the calls to Meet A Mum Association (MAMA) are from women with young babies who feel cut off from their old friends at work and are finding it hard to make new ones at home. When a woman phones MAMA, she is put in touch with another mother living nearby so they can build up friendship and support on a one to one basis. The local groups also usually arrange regular coffee meetings in each other's homes. If there is no existing group, you might even consider setting one up. MAMA can provide you with details of all the other women in your area who have been in touch in the last year. By contacting them you can get together to discuss forming a group.

Of course, if mothers at home with a young baby find life rather isolated, the same can be even more true for fathers. Some couples come to an arrangement whereby the woman returns to full-time work, while her partner takes responsibility for the child-care arrangements.

Men who have found themselves in this position often say they feel excluded by the other mothers they meet. Even so, it is worth exploring the same kind of possibilities for building your own support networks – and don't be afraid to strike up conversations with other men you see pushing buggies or tots on the swings. If you are feeling really isolated, you could start your own group for dads. Put a notice in the local library or ring up the news desk of the local paper and tell them what you are planning – you may get some free publicity.

POSTNATAL DEPRESSION

New mothers are often warned to expect the 'baby blues'. These tend to occur three or four days after the birth when women may find themselves anxious, mildly depressed or bursting into tears for no obvious reason. There is a theory that the blues are due to hormonal changes as oestrogen levels drop after childbirth, but it is equally possible that they could be caused by tiredness, discomfort or even a feeling of anti-climax after the initial excitement or euphoria. Some experts, like the birth educator Sheila Kitzinger, argue that the baby blues are a hospital-induced emotional state, and the remedy is for the woman to go home as soon as possible and get to know her own baby in circumstances under her own control.

Some women, however, find themselves slipping into a deeper kind of depression. This may affect as many as one in ten new mothers and can manifest itself in many ways. A woman may find herself having panic attacks or she may be unable to sleep at all at nights. She might feel overwhelmed by feelings of sadness or hopelessness, or she may be so numb she feels nothing at all.

She might care for her baby perfectly competently, but with a sense of just going through the motions, robot-like, feeling all the time that she is being a bad mother. Others might find it impossible to cope with even simple tasks.

Sometimes postnatal depression occurs some months after the birth. Then women may not recognise it for what it is. Fortunately, these days, health visitors and other professionals are more aware of the warning signs.

Women suffering from postnatal depression may be offered anti-depressants. Progesterone supplements may help others. Counselling may also be recommended.

WOMEN: WHAT CAN YOU DO TO HELP YOURSELF?

If you are feeling depressed it can be difficult to summon up the energy to do anything at all. But it is important to get help.

- **Make an appointment to see your GP or your health visitor.** Ask to talk to someone who has time to listen.
- **Contact the Association for Postnatal Depression.** They will send you an information pack and a small questionnaire so that they can put you in touch with another mother. It can help to talk to someone who has been through the same things as yourself – and recovered.
- **Pass on what you are told to family and friends.** It is important that they understand that you are unwell, but that with their support you will get better. This may take time, though, and being told to 'cheer up' or 'pull yourself together' won't help.
- **Stop pretending everything is fine.** When people inquire how things are going, be honest. If they offer help, ask for what you need. It may just be someone to listen, or it may be someone to do the supermarket shop for you. Many mothers with depression go through a passing phase where they dread being left alone. You may need those closest to you to organise a rota so that there is always someone you trust at hand.
- **Try to get out of the house more.** If you are feeling socially isolated you need to make new friends. Check out the section on support networks above for ideas on how to do this.
- **Work out whether you can afford paid help.** Finding a baby-sitter would help you get out without the baby once in a while. Someone to clean or iron would give you more time for yourself.

- **Reconsider your return to work.** For some women the thought of going back to work can make them feel anxious or guilty about leaving their baby. This may add to the stress they already feel and may deepen their depression. It may help to rethink your future plans. On the other hand, some women find that a return to work has positive benefits. Going back to a job they know they can do, mixing with other adults and no longer having to be responsible for childcare 24 hours a day, can be such a relief that they find it much easier to cope when they are at home.

MEN: WHAT CAN YOU DO TO HELP YOUR PARTNER?

- Encourage her to seek professional help – and go with her the first time.
- If the prescribed treatment does not suit her, encourage her to go back to the doctor and ask for it to be changed.
- Accept that this is as much an illness as any physical complaint: don't try to chivvy her out of it. You need to understand that although postnatal depression is a temporary illness, and with your help and support your partner will recover, it may take a considerable period of time before she is completely better.
- If your partner hates being left alone, organise a rota so that there is always a trusted friend or relative there with her. These feelings will pass, but it is important to give her the help she needs until she is happy to be left on her own.
- When she is feeling unwell, take over whatever childcare or domestic chores she wants to give up; when she is feeling better, let her do as much as she wants to. You may find she has patches of good and bad days. That is very common with the illness.
- Remind her often that she will get better.

6 GOING BACK TO WORK

KEEP YOUR OPTIONS OPEN

Before the baby arrives you may be sure you are definitely going to return to work, or you may be in two minds about it. After the baby is born, however, you may find your feelings have changed. This happens to many women, so it's sensible to be aware of the possibility that it may happen to you. That's why it is best to keep your options open as long as possible, and that means keeping the door open for a return to work.

If you are having doubts about returning you may, understandably, feel uncomfortable about not sharing these with your employers and colleagues. Yet, as the Maternity Alliance points out, British mothers have a pretty poor deal compared with women elsewhere, so it is important not to throw away the few rights we have.

It is also worth bearing in mind that although the number of women returning to work after having a baby is increasing (in 1988, 69 per cent of women who qualified for the statutory right to return went back to work), the number of women taking maternity leave is still small compared with general staff turnover and the problems this may cause for most employers.

In any case, many women have jobs for which they can give a month's or even a week's notice. Even if you decide during your maternity leave that you have changed your mind and you are not going back after all, you may only have cut your normal notice period by a little.

For first time mums, one of the difficulties in trying to decide in advance whether you really want to go back to work or not is that until it happens, you can't be sure what it will be like to be at home with your child. Some women find it completely fulfilling and exciting. Others miss the challenges of work and the contact with other adults.

The fact that it is so difficult to predict your reactions to full-time motherhood is one of the most important reasons for keeping your option to return open. It is no disaster to change your mind and decide not to go back after all, but it could be terrible to realise you have made a mistake after your old job has been given to someone else on a permanent basis.

So take as much time as you can before making a final decision, and make sure you know when that has to be. It is a good idea to mark up on a calendar or a wall planner any essential dates that will apply in your case, such as the date you have to confirm your return to work (if that applies) or the date when you will actually start.

If you are finding it hard to come to a decision about whether you really want to return to work or not – and at what point you will let your employer know what you are going to do – you also need to try to think ahead. Will you want to go back to work at some time – and if so, would you want to work for the same employer? If the answer is 'yes', would it be in your best interests to put them in the picture sooner, rather than later? Would a different pattern of working make a return more appealing – and if so, would your employer be open to suggestions for a change? Would just a little more time at home be the answer – and if so, would it be possible to negotiate a later return by taking unpaid leave or holidays?

WEIGHING UP THE PROS AND CONS OF WORK

Before you make a final decision it is a good idea to draw up a checklist to compare all the possible advantages and disadvantages of returning to work versus staying at home.

Only you will know what applies particularly in your circumstances, but a typical list might look like this:

Reasons for going back	Reasons for staying at home
Money for necessities	Feel guilty about leaving child
Money of one's own	Childcare costly/hard to find
Self-esteem	Enjoying motherhood
Career prospects	Unfriendly work patterns
Social contact	Not enjoying job
Enjoy job	Want more time with child

FINANCES

Once you have drawn up a list, try to examine the items on it in more detail. When you are thinking about the financial implications of staying at home v. returning to work, for example, make sure you get your sums right.

How much would you end up paying someone else to carry out the childcare you would have done for nothing, and what hidden costs might this involve? If you work, will there be extra expenses because your time will be more limited? For example, will you be spending more on cans of baby foods for your child and convenience foods for yourself if you don't have time to cook much at home?

Then there is the cost of getting to and from work, and the amount that always goes on cups of coffee, sandwiches, even office leaving presents. If you have to look smart for work, how much extra would you be spending on clothes?

On the other hand, when you work out the final figures, remember to look at the total package, not just your salary or take-home pay. Are there some job-related perks you would stand to lose: a company car, a pension scheme, discount clothes or food, cheap mortgage, health insurance?

And don't forget to look beyond the figures. If you stayed at home, at least for a while you might be able to manage financially, but what would you have to go without? And would you mind if you no longer had any money you could call your own?

"What I missed most was having some money to call my own. We had to watch what we spent and although I didn't mind spending out on things for baby I felt incredibly guilty about buying myself even a magazine. And I hated using money from the joint account to buy my husband a birthday present. He used to say I was being silly, that it was our money no matter who earned it. But it mattered to me."

Renee (28) building society cashier

SELF-ESTEEM

You also need to think about what your job really means to you. Is it an essential part of the person you are; does it help to make you feel good about yourself? Or would you feel just as fulfilled if you stayed at home. Bringing up children can be stimulating and challenging and many women find motherhood as rewarding as paid work. Others say it's important for them to spend some time outside the home being something other than a parent or a partner.

Holding down a job or climbing a career ladder can boost a woman's confidence and self esteem. Mixing with other adults can be an antidote to nappies and babytalk. On the other hand, things that once seemed very important – sales figures, performance targets, whatever – may, after the birth of a baby, pale into insignificance compared with the satisfaction you get from bringing up a happy, healthy child.

"By the time my daughter was nine months old I couldn't bear having nothing to do outside the home. I started looking for another job. It was hard to leave my daughter and to find the right person to take care of her, but it was the right decision in the end. My daughter hasn't suffered at all and I'm much happier all round."

Sara (33) accounting officer

"I fully intended to go back to work, but I felt such a rush of love for this tiny baby that I had second thoughts. It wasn't an easy choice and I knew we would be hard pushed financially if I stopped working, but my husband backed me up when I decided I wanted to stay at home after all. I feel the first couple of years are so important. I don't want to miss them."

Linda (23) sales assistant

OTHER PEOPLE

Apart from your own feelings about returning to work, you will also need to consider those of others. Your family or your partner's relatives may tell you that children need their mothers at home. Workmates may warn you that if you jump off the career ladder now, you'll never get back on.

Listen to what people say, particularly those closest to you. The final decision has to be yours, but their views may make a difference. If you decide to go back to work you will need all the support you can get at home.

If you have a partner, you may find yourself exploring issues that you haven't discussed in depth before, especially when you get down to the day-to-day practicalities of who will be doing what now that you have a child.

In an ideal world, of course, we would all sit down at the start of a relationship and discuss our hopes and expectations. In practice, our feelings often stay undefined and undisclosed, only surfacing when something else – like the arrival of a baby – makes us pay attention to more than the here-and-now.

One of the things you will need to consider is whether the balance of your relationship will change, if you are both working parents. Will one parent take the role of the primary wage-earner with the other as the primary care-giver? Or do you intend to share both roles equally? How will you split the childcare and the household chores – and if someone else is to take over when you are both at work, which of you will be responsible for setting up and managing the arrangements?

Traditionally fathers used to be responsible for earning enough money to feed, house and clothe their family, while mothers took on the responsibility for running the home and caring for the children. These days things are often very different with both parents contributing to the household finances and sharing the chores and the childcare.

What you need to discuss is not just the way in which you might do this, but the feelings you have about your role and responsibilities within the family. If one of you earns more than the other, do they feel that makes their job crucial in terms of your financial stability – and does that make it less likely, for example, that they will be willing to take time off if someone has to be at home in a crisis?

Perhaps you feel that your work is equally important to you, regardless of how much you both earn. In that case, how will you decide whose work takes precedence when one of you is needed at home?

"I didn't want Katie to give up work when we had the baby. She loved her job and in any case we needed the money. And I loved being a dad. But although we started out trying to share everything, it didn't work. For one thing, the childminder was clearly happier talking to Katie than to me and since Katie had been looking after the baby herself during her maternity leave, she still tended to do more of the caring than I did, even after she went back to work.

So we sat down and talked about it and came to an understanding. Katie's first responsibility is the baby. Her job's important but it comes second. For me, it's the other way round. We both contribute to the finances and the childcare, but the emphasis is slightly different for each of us."

Mike (39) graphic designer

When you are considering these issues, you need to take into account the attitudes you may have unconsciously absorbed during your own childhood, and the opinions you may have formed since.

How do you feel about children growing up in families where both parents work? Adults who themselves grew up in such families might see this as the norm – or they may feel they missed out during childhood. The way your family was structured is bound to influence the way you both feel.

When you are considering these issues you might also think about the possibility of reversing the traditional roles. In some families it is the father who decides to stay at home, while the mother returns to a full-time job. It may be that he is not, for one reason or another, in paid work at the time. It may be that the couple decide the mother's earning power or involvement in a career is greater.

"I'm self-employed and there wasn't much work around when Dina's maternity leave was up. Paying someone to look after the baby seemed daft, when I was around and could do it. It feels a bit odd, sometimes, being the only man at the baby clinic and I sometimes miss my mates. But I always wanted to be a hands-on dad and I can still take on the odd job for people at weekends. I think the only person who's a bit uncomfortable with the arrangement is my mum, but she's rather old-fashioned. I certainly don't feel any less of a man because I'm the one at home."

Steve (31) painter and decorator

"I was surprised when Jenny said she wanted to go back to work when our baby was six months old. I thought she'd want to stay home, like my mother did, until Ben was at least going to school. We had some pretty heated discussions, until I accepted that Jenny's job meant a lot to her and that was what she wanted to do. Ben went to a child-minder and he's been fine – and because Jenny's been working I've had to share the load at home and I think I'm closer to Ben as a result."

Robert (29) teacher

Try to investigate all the angles. Ask yourselves, 'What are the advantages for you as a couple if both of you work, and what are the disadvantages? What steps could you take to make the balance feel right?'

GUILT

Some mothers may, deep down, feel guilty about wanting to go back to work. Perhaps you feel you would be a 'better' mother if you stayed at home. Perhaps others close to you believe that, too.

Alternatively, you might feel guilty about *not* wanting to go back to work. You might feel bad about letting your bosses or colleagues down, or about not wanting to leave your baby in order to boost the family coffers. You might feel guilty about wasting the expertise you have invested so much time in developing.

The following pointers may help you make up your mind and feel happy with your final decision.

- Extra loving adults can be a bonus in a baby's life. Babies do need consistent and continuous care that allows them to build up relationships and develop as social human beings – but this need not be provided by a parent alone. In the past a baby's care was often shared between a network of elder sisters, grandparents and aunts, whether the mother worked or not.
- If working makes you happier, it will have a knock-on effect. The better you feel about yourself, the more you will enjoy the time you do spend at home. If you are not happy, you are unlikely to make your baby happy either.
- Of course, the reverse is true, too. If you feel forced into working against your wishes, you won't necessarily be sweetness and light at home.
- Feeling guilty, or angry and resentful, doesn't get you anywhere. It's good to be able to recognise those feelings, but it's important to go further than that. If you aren't happy with the way things are, change what you can. Then accept what you can't.

    For example, if you are unsure about going back to work or not, would you feel happier if you could change your work pattern? Is there a middle road that would offer a compromise between returning to the job you did before and giving up work altogether? If you have a partner, could they alter their work pattern, so that you could share more of the childcare between you, instead of having to rely on other people?

"I knew Marie was worried about how things would work out if she went back to her full-time job in an office, so I asked my boss if I could switch to early shifts. That meant I could pick the baby up from the minder. Marie got everything ready in the mornings and dropped the

baby off; I took over in the afternoons and early evenings. We found it worked for us, and I enjoyed being with the baby."

Stewart (27) security guard

ALTERNATIVES TO A FULL-TIME JOB

PART-TIME WORKING

If you are a valued employee, you might persuade your boss to keep you on on this basis without losing any seniority you might have, although part-time work is often low paid, low status. Part-time work may suit you if the hours mean your partner or a family member will look after the baby to avoid extra childcare costs. Some companies, such as Marks & Spencer and McDonald's, have developed part-time management opportunities.

It is worth knowing that although there is no positive right to return to a part-time post after maternity leave, an unjustifiable refusal to such a request may constitute unlawful indirect sex discrimination. If you are interested in going back part-time, and your employer does not agree to this, get advice from a law centre, the Citizens' Advice Bureau or the Equal Opportunities Commission.

WORKING FROM HOME

With modern technology (faxes, computers, phone-links) many office jobs can be done from home (teleworking) Sometimes it is possible to share equipment with other workers in a telecottage or a teleservice centre. Could you convince your employers that you don't have be in the work-place all the time to get your job done? A third of those employed the Digital Equipment Company, for example, now work regularly from home and a range of contracts is offered with the option of being entirely home-based.

Alternatively, some women decide to go freelance or set up their own business at home. Even at home you won't be able to work and look after a child simultaneously, so you will still need childcare (see 'Childcare options', page 112).

FLEXIBLE WORKING HOURS

This pattern of working is only flexible up to a point. Most companies have 'core hours' – usually between 10 am and 4 pm – when everyone is expected to be at work. Even so, some working parents find that being able to start work later or finish earlier than normal makes it easier to drop off or collect their child at a nursery or childminder's.

TERM-TIME WORKING

Some companies offer parents the option of term-time working. These parents are employed on the same conditions of service as other employees, but are allowed to take unpaid leave during the school holidays. One company running such a scheme is the Nationwide Building Society.

JOB-SHARING

Job-sharing can work in various ways, but essentially it means two people sharing one full-time job between them, and dividing the pay, holidays and benefits. Some job-sharers work alternate weeks, while others split the week so that each works two and a half days. Some have a system where one person works in the mornings, the other in the afternoons.

In order to job-share you may have to find someone else willing to share with you. You may have to ask around amongst your colleagues; perhaps there are others on maternity leave or who have outside interests or family commitments who would welcome the idea.

As job-sharing has become more common, a growing number of employers now have job-share policies. If yours is one, you may be able to apply to job-share even if you don't have a partner lined up. However, the easiest way of organising a job-share is to find someone else within your section or department, at the same level as you, who also wants to reduce their hours.

It is still important to start negotiating with your employer as far ahead as possible and to present a well thought-out document detailing how you think the job could be shared. Even in firms with job-share policies in place, there may be a set procedure to be followed in terms of the notice required: Leeds City Council, for example, requires three months' notice before a woman returns from maternity leave.

It may help your case to give examples of jobs, similar to yours, which are already successfully shared. The charity New Ways to Work (see 'Addresses', page 216) may be able to put you in touch with people to talk to.

You would also need to explain why job-sharing would work to the employers advantage as well as yours: you could argue that two part-timers would be more productive than one full-timer, staying energetic and creative for longer, or that two people sharing one job are likely to have different skills and expertise that would complement each other and which are unlikely to be possessed by one individual.

Because job-share applications are most successful when they are specifically tailored to a particular job within an individual organisation, you need to work out your own application. However, an excellent book on the subject, which will get you started, is *Job Sharing, A Practical Guide*, by Pan Walton, available from New Ways to Work (see 'Addresses' and 'Further reading', pages 216 and 218).

CAREER BREAKS

Again, some companies, such as Sainsbury's, allow workers to take an extended break, unpaid, of up to five years with a guaranteed job at the end of the break. Most schemes insist on you attending a few weeks' paid refresher training each year.

A PHASED RETURN

Some women negotiate a gradual return to week, phased over a month or so, starting off part-time and building up to full-time. This can give people a chance to settle their children into childcare and/or enable them to wean a breastfed baby more gradually (see page 103).

Even if your employers don't currently offer any of these options, it might be possible to negotiate a new deal. To do this, you need to arm yourself with as much information as possible. Your union, if you have one, may be able to assist you. New Ways To Work has an information service and publishes a series of booklets and factsheets on various aspects of job-sharing and other flexible work arrangements.

Once you know what you would, ideally, like, write to your employer to put forward your suggestions, so that you can discuss matters before your maternity leave runs out.

Don't forget to stress the advantages to your employer of adopting your ideas. Companies have to pay to recruit and retrain new staff, and introducing flexible patterns of working may save them money. There may be opportunities for them to get some good publicity if they adopt family-friendly policies, not to mention the creation of goodwill in the workplace and the local community.

BEFORE YOU RETURN TO WORK

If you decide you are going back to work there are a number of things you need to get organised on the home front well in advance.

You may also want to dip a toe back into the world of work before your return, to make sure you know what has been happening there. Once again it is a good idea to draw up a checklist to cover all the areas involved.

Checklist

- Childcare arrangements
- Weaning v. breastfeeding
- Division of labour
- Check out workplace

CHILDCARE ARRANGEMENTS

Ideally these should be in place soon enough to allow your child – and you – time to adjust. If possible, make the change-over a gradual one. (See page 147 for details.)

WEANING V. BREASTFEEDING

If you are still breastfeeding you will have to decide whether you want to continue, whether to introduce bottle feeds or whether you want to wean your baby altogether.

Some women decide to use a breast-pump or express milk into a sterilised bottle, which can be stored for up to 24 hours in a fridge and given to the baby when they are not there. Breast milk can also be frozen for a few weeks.

Other women carry on breastfeeding morning and evening, but decide that the baby can be offered formula milk during the day. Others switch over to bottles and formula altogether.

A number of factors may affect your decision:

- the age of your baby, and his or her appetite;
- how well breastfeeding has been established;
- how much you enjoy breastfeeding;
- how well your baby takes to a bottle;
- how difficult it will be to express and store milk once you're back at work.

If you plan to switch to bottles, at least part of the time, and you have not offered your baby a bottle before, start well before your return to work. It is probably best to avoid offering the first one when your baby is tired or irritable and needs to suck for comfort as much as to satisfy hunger. It may help if someone other than you gives the first few bottle feeds as your baby will not then be held close to your breast, smelling and anticipating breast milk. If your baby is around five or six months old you may find it easier to introduce a cup rather than a bottle. There's no rule that says you have to start with bottles first!

Your own supply of breast milk will adjust quite quickly if your baby is only bottle fed during the day. If you want to you should be able to go on breastfeeding at other times, such as first thing in the morning and in the evenings.

If you need help to carry on breastfeeding, talk to your health visitor or a breastfeeding counsellor with the NCT, or contact the

La Leche League. Your health visitor will also be able to give you advice about introducing a bottle or a cup.

"Baby books go on about how you can carry on breastfeeding after you go back to work. But the idea of expressing and storing milk seemed like too much of a hassle to me. It's sounds very idealistic, but I think you've got enough to cope with as a working mum without adding complications you can manage without. Perhaps I would have thought again if my baby hadn't taken happily to a bottle, but as it was I was able to wean him without any problems when he was six months old – just before I was due back."

Elliane (32) researcher

DIVISION OF LABOUR

Studies show that working mothers have fewer hours of leisure time than working fathers – no doubt because women still tend to be the ones who have to juggle the responsibilities of looking after the children, the house and their job.

If you have a partner it is important to sort out how you intend to manage things once you go back to work. If, for example, you have taken over some of the tasks that were once shared simply because you have been at home, you will have to discuss whether this arrangement will continue once you're working again. Even if you always did most of the household chores, you have to bear in mind that you will now have less 'free' time for housework. When you get back from work there will be a child to look after. And, of course, childcare itself is now added to all the things that the two of you had to do before.

Counsellors often find that couples spend very little time sitting down to talk through the practicalities of their life. Instead they deal with issues as they crop up – what's known in the business world as 'crisis management'. But it's much better to try and avoid conflict and crises by planning ahead and deciding who should be responsible for what and how the day-to-day practicalities of life should be allocated.

It's a good idea to have a written list that covers everything you can think of. You can subdivide it under different headings. For example you might want to include the following:

- childcare (e.g. taking to and from minder/nursery, dealing with admin, arranging for care, paying fees or wages);
- child-care at home (e.g. feeding, bathing, changing, playing, shopping for baby supplies, taking to clinic);
- housework (e.g. cleaning, tidying, bed-making;
- administration (e.g. paying bills, dealing with mail);
- gardening (e.g. care of indoor plants, mowing lawn);
- maintenance (repairs, painting and decorating);
- laundry (washing, ironing);
- meals (shopping, cooking, washing up).

Obviously, 'who does what' will depend on your own personal circumstances, on who gets home first, on what skills you each have and what jobs you both prefer doing. The situation may also be complicated by the feelings you have about the roles men and women have traditionally played. The point is that you don't have to strive for perfect equality. All you have to do is to talk it through to try to come to some kind of balance, where neither of you feels overburdened or resentful.

"I had got into the habit of relying on Annie to do more around the house. She was at home, so it didn't seem too much of an imposition to ask her to iron a few shirts or pick up my cleaning when she took the baby out for a walk. But when she went back to work she said, quite rightly, that she couldn't be expected to do two jobs and I'd have to pull my weight. She still tends to do more housework than me, but I do the supermarket shop and most of the ironing and we

both look after Charlie. I always take him to the nursery and Annie picks him up.

Callum (27) computer salesman

DIPPING A TOE BACK AT WORK

Some organisations make a point of keeping in touch with women on maternity leave, letting them know about changes that are going on or training courses being set up. If yours isn't like this, it is a good idea to make contact before you start back at work. You might like to consider some of the following:

- **Ask to be sent newsletters or copies of memos or notices** that might apply to your job.
- **Arrange to meet some of your colleagues** – at lunchtime, say – so that you can catch up on the news. It may be better to go without your baby, so make a date to coincide with the introduction of your child-care arrangements. This can be a good way of easing those in gently, too.
- **Make an appointment to see your immediate boss,** perhaps after meeting your colleagues. This is a good way to show you have sorted out your childcare arrangements and are keen to come back. Going into the workplace also lets you take note of any changes that have taken place. Then, on your first day back, you won't be thrown if the place has been reorganised since you left and you don't even know where to hang your coat!

WHEN YOU FIRST GO BACK

Going back to work may initially feel as strange as being at home all the time. Almost certainly you will have a mixture of feelings. Even if you have been looking forward to your return, you may find you miss your child more than you anticipated. You may find yourself feeling less confident, particularly if you are worrying about whether your breasts will start to leak milk or if you feel you no longer look quite as trim as you used to.

You may be wondering if you will be able to concentrate on what you are supposed to be doing, especially if you keep thinking about the baby and what you would have been doing together if you were at home.

On the other hand, some women feel guilty because they *don't* think about the baby for hours on end, simply because they find their work enjoyable and absorbing.

Your colleagues will probably be pleased to see you, but it is also possible that you may encounter some attitudes that are less welcoming. Some people may simply disapprove in principle of women returning to work while their children are young, others may envy you for having been able to take time off to have a baby and still keep your job, while some may feel resentful about any upheaval involved in covering for you while you were on leave.

In addition, you are quite likely to find yourself more tired than usual. If your baby is still waking at night you will no longer be able to catch up on your sleep by having the occasional lie-in or a cat-nap during the baby's day-time rest. Going to work imposes new time pressures on you: you can no longer set your own schedules. Instead you have to get up, get ready and get to work by a certain time. Yet at the same time the baby needs attention, too. And when you get home from work the demands on your time and your energy continue. You can't just flop – someone has to look after the baby.

WHAT CAN YOU DO TO HELP YOURSELF?

- **Learn to prioritise.** If you go back to work you will have less time to fit in all the things you used to do when you were at home. You have to decide what is most important and what can go by the board. It is not just a question of deciding which tasks take up your time, you need to think about which ones use up most of your energy. Once you have worked out what your priorities are, stick to them. Don't worry if you chose to spend time with your family at the expense of the housework. Having a happy child is more important than having a tidy home.

- **Get organised.** It helps if you plan ahead so that everyone knows what is meant to be happening when. Keep a planner somewhere handy – on the kitchen wall, for example – and make sure everyone fills in important dates and events. You might want to back this up with a folder where you can keep all the notes that come home from nursery, school, or any other group you are involved with. Then you will know where to find the details about the end of term concert or the trip to the zoo.

- **Make lists.** Don't rely on your memory. If you are busy or under pressure it may let you down.

- **Learn to delegate.** If you have been used to running the home you may feel guilty about asking others to lend a hand. Equally, you may find it hard to stand back and watch someone else doing what you used to do, differently. Feelings like these are understandable, but if you can't relinquish some of your domestic responsibilities you may end up feeling stressed and miserable – and that won't help anyone in the long run.

- **Learn to say 'no'.** If people are used to you being available whenever you are needed, you may have to develop new techniques to avoid taking on more than you can really cope with. Look at the section on assertiveness. If you can, practise what you will say, firmly and calmly, before the time comes.

- No, I can't help get ready for the bring and buy
- No, I can't take you swimming on Saturday morning, you'll have to get the bus
- No, I can't wash out your football kit right now

You don't have to give explanations – if you do, you are more likely to get drawn into a debate. If your refusal upsets the other person you can acknowledge their feelings, but stick to your guns.

- I'm sorry you feel cross with me, but I can't take you swimming.

The more you practise, the easier it gets.

- **Accept that it is normal to have mixed feelings.** Any change is usually difficult to cope with but if you give yourself time to adjust to the new pattern you will probably begin to feel less stressed.
- **Try to discover what lies behind your feelings** and then see if there is any action you could take. Would it help to change the childcare arrangements? Would you feel better if you were able to ring your carer at a set time during the day?
- **It may help to talk to other women at work** who have been through the same experiences.
- **If you are worried about leaking breasts,** wear patterned tops and keep a supply of breast pads handy. Your milk supply will soon adjust.
- **Keep the situation under review.** If, after a while, it is clear that things are not working think about your choices. There is nothing wrong with changing your mind.

"I arranged for the baby to go to a childminder when I went back to work. But although I knew my baby was safe and well cared for, I didn't think she was getting the kind of stimulation she needed. No

matter when I rang, the minder was always there and you could hear the television on. They never seemed to go out for walks or even up to the shops. In the end I decided to start looking for a nursery place. It's more expensive, but I feel better about it, and it's made a huge difference to how much I feel I can concentrate at work."

Cheryl (34) tax officer

"I went back to work as planned when the baby was six months old. I'd always enjoyed my job but my heart just wasn't in it and n the end I handed in my notice. I will probably look for another job when she starts nursery next year but now I'm really enjoying her and although money's tight I don't regret changing my mind."

Caroline (25) telesales

7 CHILDCARE OPTIONS

One of the most consuming of issues for working parents is how to find high quality and affordable childcare for their children while they are at work. There's no evidence that children need to be looked after exclusively by their parents. What's important is that care is high quality and consistent, and that arrangements fit in as easily as possible with your day-to-day life to avoid unnecessary stress. Ask any working mother: everything seems to depend on childcare working smoothly. If arrangements are unsatisfactory or look like breaking down, stress levels soar. Your child may pick up your concerns and lose confidence too. You need to be able to depend on the arrangement you have, and feel comfortable with it.

Parents naturally want the best for their children, but the reality is that there's a lack of childcare in the UK, and a lot of parents find themselves with little or no choice about the childcare they use. The National Childcare Campaign was established in 1980 and is a pressure group campaigning for flexible, diverse, publicly-subsidised childcare. It provides information to parents who themselves wish to campaign. There's no such thing as the ideal type of care. Finding the right solution for you is a question of balancing your own needs and those of each of your children with what is practically available. At any one time, this will throw up a unique combination of factors, depending on how many children you have, their ages, where you live and work, your hours of work, the flexibility and demands of your job, your network of family and friends locally, whether you have a partner and how much they are able to help. It's no good finding the 'perfect' childminder if she lives the other side of town, reached via two difficult bus journeys and in the opposite direction from your work!

It really comes down to matching practical considerations with your priorities about the childcare you are looking for, going with what's available and in the end coming out with something that works for you. Whatever type of care you choose, the quality of the provision will vary from person to person and place to place. There are good and bad childminders, good and bad nannies, good and bad day nurseries. You need to check the quality of care your child is receiving.

Demand for childcare services is growing all the time; the majority of mothers now work, including around half of those with pre-school children, many of whom work part-time. Child-care needs don't end when your children go to school – if anything they get more complex, and may continue well into teenage years. So what are your childcare options? This chapter considers the different types of childcare that may be available to you, depending on where you live, how much you can afford to pay, the policies of your local authority or employer, and private or voluntary sector provision nearby. It will help you to weigh up what care, or possibly patchwork of care, will suit your family's needs best, and point you to ways of finding it. Perhaps most important, it highlights some features of high quality childcare.

CARE IN THE HOME FOR UNDER-FIVES

You may want to find someone to care for your child in a home setting, either yours or theirs, involving a single familiar carer who will look after your own children either exclusively or with a small number of others. This may be most like the care you provide when you're at home, as opposed to the more hectic environment of group care, where your child will mix with a lot of children and a number of different carers.

There are several options to consider, although the age of your child and the amount you can afford to pay may well rule out some of the possibilities. The key providers of home care are family and friends, childminders, mothers helps, nannies and au-pairs (au-pairs are included here because they provide home care, but are more suitable for over-fives) and each of these are considered here.

FAMILY AND FRIENDS

Around 40 per cent of pre-school children are cared for by a member of the family other than a parent – often a grandparent – or by a friend or neighbour. This may seem the simplest way to solve your childcare needs, and because it is often unpaid or cheap it may be all you can afford. You may feel anxious about leaving your children, especially a first child, in the care of a stranger, whereas family and friends will be known to you and your child and may share common values with you.

Of course, families can only help out regularly if they live close to you, and this is less likely than was once the case as people move around to find work opportunities. But even if your mum lives round the corner, you shouldn't assume that she wants the responsibility of caring for your children, however much she dotes on them. She may have other commitments, including a job of her own, or perhaps doesn't want to be tied down at a time when she was looking forward to new opportunities and freedom; maybe she's not fit enough to cope with the physical demands of young children, although she may be reluctant to admit this.

While grandparents may welcome the chance to see more of their grandchildren, and friends may seem enthusiastic about taking on your children, tensions can arise if you overstep boundaries and make too many demands, or if they have ways of doing things that you aren't happy with. Sometimes it's harder with family and friends to let them know how you want things done and to lay down certain rules and patterns; for example, they may give your children too many sweet foods, give in to them too easily when they have a tantrum, or expect more sensible behaviour than can reasonably be expected of a three year old.

Using a friend to look after your children can work well as long as you know her well enough to be able to depend on her, and are both clear about the arrangements. Sometimes it can lead to the end of what seemed like a good relationship! If you work part-time, you may be able to reciprocate childcare with a friend rather than paying – you have their children when you're at home, and vice versa. If more than two families are involved, you will need to be registered (see page 145). This may be a particularly workable arrangement if your children are similar ages and enjoy playing together but remember that children fall in and out of friendships very easily, and there may be days when they are daggers drawn! The disadvantage is that it puts more pressure on you. When you're not at work, you will have the added responsibility of caring for other children, and you won't be able to give your own child so much undivided attention. You'll also have less time for other household chores that have to be fitted in to the limited time you have at home.

Whether you use your mum or other family member or a friend, it's important to talk through all the details carefully and for everyone involved to be clear about what the expectations are:

- **Where will the care take place:** in your home, with all the usual playthings; or in their home so they can get on with their own housework and other routines?
- **Will they take your child to local activities:** mother and toddler clubs, playgroup, toy library, so they begin to socialise with other children?
- **Will you pay them the going rate or reciprocate by helping them out too?** If not, will you feel forever in their debt?
- **Will it be possible to talk through problems** and be open with each other if things don't seem to work out?
- **What will happen when your child, or your friend's child, is ill?**
- **How will you work out holiday times to suit everyone?**

With careful planning, it can turn out to be an ideal arrangement all round:

"My mum was over the moon when her first grandchild arrived, and more than happy to take on looking after her when I went back to work part-time after six months. At first I took Lucy to mum's on my way to work, but later it was more convenient for mum to come to us and have all Lucy's toys and equipment around! It was a great arrangement, mainly because we're very close and see eye to eye on most things. I always paid her the going rate – I knew what marvellous value I was getting."

Diana (26) hairdresser

"My friend offered to mind my daughter when I went back to work. She has a little girl the same age, and they go to the same playgroup and ballet class. I knew she'd be safe and happy there. We wanted to do it properly so Jane applied to social services and it was just a formality for her to become registered."

Paula (29) office administrator

CHILDMINDERS

A childminder is someone who looks after children in her own home for payment. Your child will be cared for in a family environment, with many of the experiences they would have at home, like shopping and helping with cooking. There will probably be other children there to play with, and if you have more than one child it's often possible for them to be cared for together right through to the beginning of school and beyond. Many childminders are themselves mothers, either caring for their own young children alongside yours, or with older children. Either way, they are likely to have experience of children.

Finding a childminder

Start looking for a childminder as early as possible – perhaps while you are still pregnant – in order to get a good, local one. Childminders have to be registered with social services (see page 145) so your local department should have a list, although it may not be completely up to date. Phone and ask for the person who deals with under-eights. If the first childminders you visit are not what you are looking for, do ask them for more names; even if the childminder is not quite so close to where you live, you'll probably prefer a slightly longer journey for a childminder you like and trust.

Besides social services, you may hear of a childminder at your doctor's surgery or child clinic, or through a friend. You could advertise in a newsagent or local paper, or at the local school. If you want to use someone, a friend perhaps, who is not already registered, she can apply for registration very easily (see page 145).

You could also look for a childminder through a childminding organisation. The National Childminding Association can put you in touch with your local organisation or childminders with vacancies in your area.

Choosing a childminder

Visit a number of childminders and find out as much as you can about the sort of care they will provide for your child before making a final choice. As well as their personal qualities, you need to find someone who is available for the days and hours you require, and who lives in a convenient place for your home and work. If you have more than one child, you will probably want someone with vacancies for each of them, perhaps including after school and holiday care for older children.

Make an appointment to see the childminder in her own home. It helps to have a list of things you want to ask and look out for:

- **What does she charge?** (See below.)
- **What training or experience does she have** (including her own children), **and is she registered?**
- **Can she work hours to fit in with your work commitments?**
- **Will she provide interesting activities** in a safe environment, with plenty of room, a variety of toys, limited TV programmes, messy play activities and a garden?
- **Does she seem patient, child-centred, and not too house proud?**
- **How many other children will she care for** at the same time as yours, and how old are they?
- **Will she take your child out** to shops and the park, to groups or activities such as a playgroup or swimming class, to the baby clinic or to and from school?
- **Will she provide healthy meals and snacks** and not too many sweet foods and drinks? If you need to drop your child early,

will she provide breakfast? Should you supply baby milk and food?

- **Does she have similar ideas to you about childrearing:** for example, potty training or dealing with tantrums?
- **Is there somewhere for your child to have a nap?**
- **Is it a non-smoking environment?**
- **How will you co-ordinate holiday arrangements?**

You will probably want to visit her more than once, taking your child along to see how they respond to each other, and seeing her in action with other children she cares for. You will be able to pick up how happy and stimulated they seem.

"I went to see a childminder who had been recommended by social services. I didn't particularly warm to her, and noticed that she directed all her attention to me, hardly bothering to speak to my daughter. Her home was very tidy, too. The next lady I went to see seemed much more interested in children – she took Helen into the garden to see her rabbits. She was very happy to be flexible about days because she only cared for two other children, and that suited my irregular work commitments."

Pamela (29) journalist

How much will it cost?

You may pay an hourly, daily or weekly rate, depending how regular your work pattern is. Fees vary quite a bit from place to place, ranging from £50 to £90 a week. Sometimes you can get a reduction for a second child.

There are few hidden costs with childminders, apart from the cost of getting your child there. Find out whether your childminder will charge the full rate or a retainer when your child is away because of illness or holiday. Compared with care in your own home, you will not have to pay for heating, food, wear and tear or other expenses, and your home will be as tidy as when you left it.

If your income is very low, you may be able to get help with your child minding fees from the council (depending on where you live), contributing a proportion of your earnings.

NANNIES AND MOTHER'S HELPS

Both nannies and mother's helps will come to your home, but offer different sorts of help and experience.

A mother's help is usually young and fairly inexperienced, and will give you a hand with light cleaning, shopping and cooking as well as helping to look after your children, but will not usually have sole charge. If you work only short hours, or perhaps do some work from home and want some extra help with housework and children, a mother's help may be a good choice. Or you may find that the mother's help you employ while you're on maternity leave develops into your nanny. She can build up experience while you are at hand to help out with any problems, and when it comes to the time for you to return to work, you may feel confident enough to leave her in charge.

"When Tom was born, I knew I'd be pushed to cope with three under-fours, but was lucky to be able to afford to employ a mother's help. Lesley was 17, and had worked as an au-pair in Germany for a year. She was an absolute godsend – arriving early morning to help with the chaos of breakfast and dressing while I fed and bathed the baby, helping with housework and playing with the girls until lunchtime, then having the afternoon off and returning to help out with the hurly-burly of children's tea, supper, bathtime, bedtime. It meant I could devote some time to the girls without the distractions of a screaming baby.

After six months I went back to work part-time, and Lesley took over. By then she had become a trusted nanny-come-mothers-help and felt like one of the family. She stayed with us until Tom started school. She's remained a close friend to us all, and the children still enjoy seeing her."

Mary (37) writer

A nanny will look after your children in your own home, doing anything related to their care, including preparing their meals, washing and ironing their clothes, and delivering them to birthday parties, but usually excluding general housework. She may have a qualification related to looking after children (see 'Training and qualifications', page 142), or several years' experience working with young children.

It's true that nannies are one of the most expensive of the childcare options, and yet they are no longer exclusively for the royal or otherwise privileged, and if you have two or more children to be cared for while you work, a nanny may well be a viable alternative. To make it cheaper, you could consider sharing a nanny (see page 127). These days a live-in nanny will live as part of the family, expect to be treated as a professional in her own right, wear clothes of her own choosing rather than the uniforms of days gone by, and have a life of her own outside work hours.

"I felt embarrassed admitting to people that we had a nanny – I thought they'd think us either extremely rich, which we certainly weren't, or stuck up, or both. The truth was that most of my salary went to the nanny while I was still building my career as a solicitor, but I was happy with that in exchange for the peace of mind it gave me to know that the children were so well looked after."

Linda (30) solicitor

Live in or out?
Nannies and mother's helps may live in or out, and there are certain advantages and disadvantages to each. Before deciding

which might suit you best, it may help to think through the following issues:

- **Do you have a bedroom to spare, enough space generally** so that you will not be living on top of each other, and will bathroom facilities be over-stretched in the mornings?

- **Will you mind the lack of privacy involved with having someone living in your home?** What about evenings and weekends? Might it be possible to find someone to live in during the working week only?

- **Your household expenses including food and fuel will be higher if you have someone living-in, but you will not have to pay such high wages compared to someone who lives out.** You may need to heat an additional room, or your home for longer periods if they are at home when you are usually out; you will get through more hot water; your telephone bill will almost certainly be larger, especially if they make a lot of peak-time calls. It's best to come to an agreement about whether they will pay for these. An itemised bill will help you identify calls.

- **Would you welcome having someone on tap for babysitting, or prefer having evenings at home in privacy?** With live-in help, it doesn't matter how late you get home from an evening out – they can just go to bed.

- **With live-in help you won't have to worry about them turning up late in the morning,** and pressures on you to get home on time will be less though you should be careful not to abuse this. It may be especially useful if your job involves long, unpredictable hours or perhaps takes you away from home overnight.

- **The older the carer, the less likely they are to want to forfeit their independence by living in.** But live-in carers are likely to stay longer, and you'll probably get plenty of notice if they intend leaving.

Finding a mother's help/nanny

Advertising: If you're looking for live-in help, you could advertise in a national magazine such as *The Lady* or *Nursery World* or respond to adverts placed there by nannies looking for work. For someone to live out, you may be better off advertising in your local papers, job-centres, shop windows, libraries or health clinics.

You should state the duties and hours of work involved, qualifications, experience and references required, whether the job involves 'sole charge' or back-up help, the number and ages of your children, any special needs such as cooking, housework, non-smoker, driving licence, or preferred ages; and for live-in help, the accommodation you will provide, including for example own TV. Give a contact phone number and when you can be reached there, or a box number for written applications.

Word of mouth: Talk to friends and neighbours about the sort of person you're looking for. Your friends' nannies may be part of a local 'nanny network' and know of someone looking for work.

Local colleges: Colleges running NNEB or other relevant courses (see page 143) may be a good source of newly trained people or temporary help over holiday periods.

Agencies: Specialist agencies are listed in Yellow Pages, or may advertise in magazines like *Nursery World* and *The Lady*. They will help you find a daily or live-in mother's help or nanny, and are often a good source of temporary help to fill a stop-gap or emergency. They may charge a fixed fee or percentage of salary (you can expect to pay a fee of anything between £200–£300) in return for which they will try to match your requirements with available staff on their books. They will send you details of one or more suitable applicants, and once you've made an initial selection they will check out qualifications and references for you (you may still want to satisfy yourself about these), and help fix up an interview. The agency may well follow up that all is well after your carer starts work, and if things don't work out and she leaves very quickly, you should get part or all of the fee refunded, or a replacement free of charge.

Interviewing

You may feel nervous about interviewing people for a job, but remember that they will probably be just as anxious as you. An interview will allow you to find out more about their personal and work experience and their views on different aspects of looking after young children. You'll be able to get a feeling about how closely their approach fits in with your own, and whether you'll be happy to leave your child in their care. The interview will also allow you to give plenty of information about your needs – hours and days of work, activities they will be required to take your child to, details of duties that will be involved, pay, and holiday arrangements.

Introduce your children during the interview, see how they relate to and talk with them, and how they respond to each other. Older children may have their own views about the people you interview, but should not be given the overall responsibility of deciding as they will not be able to make a rational choice. It helps to prepare some questions to ask, and also give them the chance to ask you things. Think through how you will find out about:

- **their training and qualifications;**
- **their experience of caring for children,** what ages they were, how many, whether they had sole charge, what hours they worked;
- **how long they have worked in their present job,** and why they are leaving;
- **the things which they enjoy most about caring for young children,** and what they find most difficult;

- **what sort of activities they would organise for the children:** creative play, reading, visits to parks, libraries, help with cooking and so on;
- **how closely their views of child rearing tie in with your own:** for example, their views on potty training, healthy diets, tantrums;
- **practical details** such as any difficulties they might have getting to you on time, whether they drive, whether they are happy with the duties you have identified.
- **what they would do in an emergency;**
- **references:** as well as two written references, check that they are happy for you to speak to a previous employer on the phone for more detailed feedback.

At the end of the interview, it's fine to tell them that you are seeing some other applicants, and that you will be able to let them know by a certain day. If you have a partner, it's preferable to interview together but if that's not possible, you may want to shortlist down to one or two, and then invite them back to meet your partner or to have another chance to meet them yourself before making a final decision.

Agreeing terms and conditions

You will need to agree on the terms and conditions of the job, including the duties involved, hours of work, pay, holidays, what happens when they're sick, notice of leaving on both sides, and so on. In order to avoid misunderstandings it helps to draw up a written contract outlining the basic details:

- **Duties:** These will mainly be looking after your children and playing with them, but may also include cooking their meals and washing up, tidying children's rooms and elsewhere in the house, sorting out toys, washing and ironing their clothes and bedding, taking them on outings or to playgroup, school, cubs or other activities. You can negotiate too for evening babysitting, but give plenty of notice and remember they have a social life too.

- **Hours:** Whether your nanny or mother's help lives in or out, they will expect set hours. These may vary from day to day but need to be agreed by you both, and kept to as nearly as possible. If your children are at school and you employ a nanny part-time, think about what you'll do in school holidays or when your child is away from school ill (see 'Contingency plans', page 157).

- **Pay:** How much you pay will depend on qualifications and experience, and where you live. You won't normally have to pay extra for more than one child of your own, but if you share a nanny with another family then the nanny will expect more (see 'Sharing a nanny', page 127). Because rates of pay vary widely and date quickly, it's not helpful to specify them here, but you can find out about current pay from other local mothers with nannies, or from nanny agencies.

- **Tax and NI:** If you pay more than a certain amount each week you will have to deduct income tax (under Pay As You Earn); National Insurance (NI) contributions and employer's NI contributions have to be paid on income over a certain amount. You can send this to the Inland Revenue quarterly. The organisation Nannytax provides advice and a payroll service for parents employing a nanny. Some nannies are able to get self-employed status and pay their own tax and NI.

For example, at 1993-94 rates (weekly):

Net pay received by your nanny	£120.00
Income Tax	£ 17.36
NI contributions	£ 10.19
Employer's NI contributions	£ 11.21
Total cost to you	**£158.76 a week**

Net pay received by your nanny	£200.00
Income Tax	£ 48.11
NI contributions	£ 22.49
Employer's NI contributions	£ 27.59
Total cost to you	**£298.19 a week**

- **Holidays:** Decide how much paid holiday you can offer. If she is willing to co-ordinate her holiday times with yours, you will not have to organise or pay for alternative care, and may be happy to pay her as usual for the weeks you take.

Sharing a nanny

If you don't need a full-time nanny, or want to reduce the cost of one, you could consider sharing. If you work certain hours or days, you could team up with another family whose hours dovetail with yours, so that the nanny makes up her full-time hours by working for each family separately. A full-time share means finding another local family, and employing a nanny between you to look after all your children together. In this case you will need to think through:

- **How will you find a family to share with?** You may know someone already, or could advertise locally, contact your local NCT group, or find out about local nanny share registers. You may have a nanny already who is willing to be shared, or may find a family first and then advertise together for a nanny.
- **Where will the children be cared for?** If it's always one home, there will be extra wear and tear, and the cost of food, heating and so on, but the nanny may do washing, ironing and tidying. If you swap around, this will be shared out better.
- **Are the children of compatible ages to make them easy to cope with,** and will they play together?
- **How will your nanny get out and about?** Will you need double buggies, additional car seats? Will she still be able to deliver your child to their usual activities?

- **How will you co-ordinate holidays to suit everyone?**
- **What will happen when one family withdraws from the arrangement,** and what notice should each of you and the nanny give.

AU-PAIRS

Au-pairs are young girls (usually 17 to 23) who come to this country from abroad and live as part of a family in return for domestic duties up to an agreed number of hours a day. Often they come to improve their English and they may want to enrol at a local college to study English as a second language. If this is so, their domestic duties will need to fit around their classes, which are typically a couple of hours a day, either morning or afternoon, four days a week.

Au-pairs may come here for anything from a few weeks to a year or more. You may be able to find one to cover just the summer holidays, or longer term. They are not able to provide full-time childcare – they work a maximum of five to six hours a day, with the possibility of two afternoons a week on top of that. There are a number of things to consider when deciding whether to use an au-pair for childcare, especially with pre-school children:

- **They are usually young and therefore relatively inexperienced.** You will need to judge for yourself how much responsibility they can be given. They lack training and qualifications relevant to childcare, and may have little or no experience of looking after children, beyond babysitting.
- **Their command of English is usually not fluent,** which may be a particular problem with very young children who are just learning to talk or who need to be able to relate closely with their carer.
- **This may be compounded by the fact that au-pairs do not usually stay very long** – often only a few months – and

frequent changes may be difficult for young children to cope with.

Au-pairs may be suitable to look after older children, say from six or seven upwards, who need care before and after school, and perhaps for longer during school holidays. They will be around to help with the morning rush, walk your children to school (or drive if they have a licence and you are happy to trust them with your children and car), and fit in some housework during the day as well as possibly attending college, before collecting the children from school and looking after them until you return from work. They will also be prepared to make a simple evening meal for themselves and the children. Their duties usually also include two or three nights babysitting a week (if you have the energy to go out that often!).

"We've used au-pairs for five or six years now – since Sam first went to school, and the girls were six and eight. Most of them have fitted in very well as part of the family, and have been responsible in the way they look after the children.

We have had a few horrors too! One girl arrived on a Saturday and announced she was homesick and going home the next Tuesday, so we had to start all over again looking for a replacement and struggling without help in the meantime. Another spent all her time in front of the TV and not bothering much to get to know the children.

On balance, though, they have worked very well, giving me the flexibility to work quite long and irregular hours, and widening the children's experience of different people and languages."

Jo (35) journalist

Finding and choosing an au-pair

There are agencies who specialise in placing au-pairs with families, and you can find these in your phone directory. Some agencies have links with particular countries, so if you are interested in one nationality you may need to choose the appropriate agency. Some of the more common countries supplying au-pairs to the UK are Spain, Denmark, Holland, Germany and France, but there is also an increasing number of girls from Eastern European countries such as Czechoslovakia and Romania, and from further afield.

The agency will help to match your needs with a suitable applicant. They provide some kind of vetting service, getting applicants to complete a registration form and writing a letter of introduction to prospective families giving information about themselves, their family background, experience with children, interests and so on. They may also ensure that references are provided. The agency will ask you about your children, home, the sort of duties they will have, your hours of work, and anything else you require such as a non-smoker or driver. You will be asked to select from the different girls you are offered, and write to her about your family, enclosing one or two family photos.

Because it is rarely possible to meet prospective au-pairs before you agree to have them, there is an element of uncertainty about whether you and your children will take to them. They will be just as anxious to choose the right family, so it's important to give each other as much information as possible. Don't try to impress them with half truths about your home or way of life – they will soon discover the reality when they arrive, and are less likely to settle well or be happy with you if they have been misled.

It's difficult to make a judgement about someone based on the little information you have. Important things to consider are:

- **Do they show evidence of being mature and responsible,** (regardless of their age)?
- **Have they ever been away from home before** so they're less likely to be homesick?

- **Have they helped with housework and childcare** (perhaps younger siblings or neighbours' children) at home? Sometimes a youngest child may find it hard to be the oldest in your family.
- **Have they shown they can cope with the responsibility of paid work** (even part-time or a Saturday job)?
- **Do they fit your needs** in terms of non-smoking, liking animals (if you have pets), being able to drive, wanting to stay the appropriate time, good use of English?
- **Do they want to go to college to improve their English?** If so, this will affect the hours they are available to work for you, but on the other hand will be a good way for them to make friends and settle.

Once you've found someone you feel will suit you, it helps to speak on the phone to get to know each other a little more, and make arrangements about when and where they will arrive. This is also a good way to find out how good their English is – make some allowances because they will probably be nervous. It's better to be clear about everything at this stage than to find there are problems once they arrive, with all the upheaval involved in replacing them.

How much will it cost?

An au-pair may seem like a very cheap way to meet certain childcare needs, being paid pocket money depending on hours and duties (see below). You should also take account of some hidden costs involved (see page 122). They are not liable for social security contributions, and therefore cannot claim sickness benefits, but they may obtain NHS treatment if they need medical attention.

- **Demi-pair:** Duties three hours a day, five days a week; general housework (vacuuming, ironing, making beds), maximum three evenings' babysitting a week; two complete free days, every afternoon and most evenings free. Pocket money: £20 per week.

- **Au-pair:** Duties five to six hours a day, five days a week; general housework; may also be available to help with children's tea and bathtime and help prepare and clear away evening meal; maximum three evenings babysitting a week; two complete free days plus some evenings. Pocket money: £35 per week.

- **Au-pair plus:** Duties same as au-pair, plus additional duties helping with children two to three afternoons a week. Pocket money: as for au-pair plus £5 extra per afternoon.

GROUP CARE FOR UNDER-FIVES

Group care can be a positive experience for children, providing an environment and range of experiences that would be difficult to emulate at home. Barbara Tizard, in *The Care of Young Children* (Thomas Coram Research Unit, 1986), suggests that even very young children can benefit from being part of a social network such as that provided by group care, which includes adults other than their parents, as well as peers and younger and older children. It's important that they are cared for in a familiar and safe environment that provides positive experiences so that they are able to face future separations with confidence.

DAY NURSERIES

These may be local authority, private, workplace, or voluntary sector, or sometimes a combination of these (for instance, a voluntary group joining with local employers and the local authority to set up a nursery). They usually offer full-day care for a large age range, sometimes from babies through to five years, but more often from two years up. They are staffed by trained nursery nurses plus trainees and other helpers, and the ratio of staff to children is laid down within the Children's Act, and varies depending on the ages of the children (see page 144). Young babies require more staff to care for them, and it is often difficult to get a place for babies under one. Your child will have other children to mix with; usually they are placed in small groups of similar ages so that they have more in common. All day nurseries must be registered by the local authority to ensure a certain standard of care and facilities. For many parents, nursery care may appeal more than home-based care for their child because they feel it is more regulated, and there are more toys, equipment, varied activities and other children than would be possible in a home environment.

Finding a day nursery

Day nurseries often have long waiting lists for places, so you should start looking and put your name down early – even before your baby is born. In some areas, places in local authority nurseries may be reserved for children with special needs. You can find out if you are eligible for a place by approaching your own local authority. If not, they will pass you on to voluntary or private day nurseries in your area. You may also find nurseries advertised in Yellow Pages or your local paper, or you could talk to friends, mothers who live nearby, your family doctor or health visitor. If your employer provides nursery care, either on-site or in partnership with other local providers, then you should put your name down for a place when you go on maternity leave, or when you start employment there (see 'Family-friendly' employers, page 7). Of course, fathers can also make use of any childcare facilities available through their workplace. If your employers don't provide childcare you could find out about other local employers who may have spare places.

You need to think about the advantages and disadvantages of using a nursery close to where you work rather than near your home. It may mean you are able to visit your child during your lunch-break, possibly allowing you to breastfeed for longer than would otherwise be possible. Think through the logistics of getting to and from work: if you have to travel far, say on crowded public transport, you may not relish the thought of doing so with your child in tow!

Choosing a day nursery

You will want to visit the nursery to find out about the sort of care and facilities offered, and to get a feel for the place. Ask about the number and ages of children cared for, how many staff there are, and what training and experience they have. You may want to ask if the involvement of parents is welcomed, either in practical ways (see, for example, 'Settling your child', page 147), or in having a say about how things are organised – perhaps through a staff/ parent advisory group. Check practical details: will the hours of opening fit in with your work schedule, including travel time; is it open all year round or closed for fixed holidays; what kind of food is provided, and can your child take a packed lunch if you prefer; is there somewhere for them to have a nap?

Ensuring quality group care

For children of different ages, you may place more importance on different aspects of group care, but research points to four key areas that are most likely to be important positive influences on children's social and intellectual development. To check out the quality of care on offer, find out about:

- **The physical environment:** It's not so much the overall number of toys or square feet of space that counts, but rather the quality and types of play and educational material available, and the way space is organised. Here are some questions to ask yourself as you look round:

- Is the space well organised into small areas, each focusing on an individual activity such as construction toys, dressing up, painting, and so on?
- Are there plenty of each type of play material, so that children are less likely to fight over toys and are encouraged in concentrated play?
- Are there several small rooms rather than an open plan area, encouraging more adult-child interaction rather than contact between staff?
- Is there a garden or nearby park that the children can use?

- **Workers:** High quality care depends on the relationship which workers are able to develop and sustain with children, and no amount of toys or marvellous facilities can replace that. Children's emotional and intellectual development is helped most by having familiar carers who they can become attached to and who respond positively to them – smiling, being accepting and non-judgemental, and being intellectually stimulating by listening, answering questions, and giving reasons and explanations. Where young children are developing language, it's especially important that their relationship with a carer is close enough for them to want to try out words, and for the carer to understand what they are saying and respond appropriately. Some nurseries have a keyworker system which means each child gets regular care from one worker where possible.

  Where workers are trained in child development and experienced in working with children, they are more likely to provide high quality care. Low staff turnover, achieved through good employment conditions and opportunities for training and development, will help foster familiarity and attachment between children and their carers.

  - Are there plenty of staff available to be involved in individual activities with small groups of children, like looking at books, doing jigsaws, or using climbing equipment?

– Is there a keyworker scheme in operation?

• **Group size:** High staff to child ratios are beneficial, and it also helps to have similar aged children within a group. Minimum staffing levels are specified as part of the Children's Act (see page 144). Small groups are likely to be more intellectually demanding, and offer the chance for sustained conversations with children individually. Children are also more likely to form lasting relationships with each other in a small group.

• **Activities:** Activities need to match a child's stage of development and individual personality. They should aim to offer educational experiences as well as helping children learn to interact well with other children and develop social skills. Children need to learn both to comply with the basic framework on offer and to develop self-direction.

– Are there plenty of free-play opportunities, with co-operation rather than confrontation in the interactions between workers and children?

– Do the activities and materials provided ensure equal opportunities for boys and girls, for children from different ethnic, linguistic and cultural backgrounds, and for children with disabilities. For example, do the books and visual materials available portray stereotyped images and messages, are both boys and girls encouraged in the full range of activities, and so on?

How much will it cost?

This will vary greatly depending on the type of nursery. Some local authority nurseries are free (usually only to children from high-need families), or you may pay a proportion of your income. Workplace nurseries are usually subsidised. Private nurseries are dearer – you may expect to pay around £80–£130 for a full week.

A DAY IN THE LIFE OF A DAY NURSERY

Woodlands Nursery in Woodford Green, Essex, is open from 7.45 am to 6.30 pm, 51 weeks of the year for children from two to five years. Four-year old Bina and her two-year old brother, Tanvier, attend for four full days a week. This is a diary recording the main features of a typical day for them:

6.30 am   Tanvier wakes and has a beaker of milk in his cot.

7 am   Bina starts to dress herself while Tanvier has his nappy changed and is washed and dressed.

7.30 am   Some hurried honey toast and juice, coats on and into the car.

7.55 am   Arrive at the nursery, change their shoes and hang their coats up on their pegs. Bina shows her mum a collage she did yesterday. Nicola, who's in charge of the nursery, takes the chance to tell Mrs. P how well Tanvier is settling in.

8.15 am   As children arrive, they go to the 'messy play area' and those who want it have breakfast. Today it's Bina's favourite cereal, but Tanvier prefers to play with the crayons.

9 am   Children go to the quiet room where Sally and Rachel organise them in a circle and go through the weather chart and news. Rachel reads a favourite story, and the children join.

9.30 am   Group time where children follow a programme of pre-school work including drawing, letters and writing. Bina joins her group (with other four to five year olds) to do a planned activity, forming letters and colouring in some worksheets on this month's theme of 'Colour and light'. Today they're learning about Diwali and Guy Fawkes. Tanvier has fun in the two to three years group with six other children, drawing round templates and colouring-in. There are three nursery workers to help the children, and Jane spends time with Tanvier and another boy, Nick, who also comes most mornings. She takes Tanvier to change his nappy.

10.30 am   All the children go to the 'messy area' for juice, then get their coats and shoes on and go out in the garden. Tanvier pushes a truck for a bit and then crawls through the plastic tunnel. Jane helps him zip his coat up. Bina is playing with her friend Amy with the hoops, and has a go on the trampoline.

11.30 am   Time to go in again, change shoes, wash hands and have a story and some songs. Bina gets picked to do the actions for 'Incy-wincy spider'.

11.50 am   Lunch: it's sausage, mashed potatoes and beans today, followed by fruit salad. All the children clean their teeth – Tanvier needs a bit of help. Then he and a few of the other very young ones go for a sleep in the quiet room on mattresses. Meanwhile, Bina is playing with her friends in the messy area, with lots of things to choose from. Some of the children are collected now and go home.

2.00 pm   The little ones are woken. It's group time for everyone again. Tanvier is enjoying playing in the home corner; Bina is busy making some special Diwali foods.

3.00 pm	It's raining hard now so instead of playing in the garden, the children do music and movement. Bina doesn't want to be a rain forest, but does her own thing instead.
3.45 pm	Wash hands and tea: a sandwich, biscuit and juice.
4.00 pm	There's story time in the quiet room but the children are rather hard to settle so a game of musical statues is organised. Tanvier sits on Nicola's knee and watches. Then he sees his mum; she helps him and Bina get their coats and shoes on, and they say goodbye.

PLAYGROUPS AND NURSERY CLASSES

These mainly offer very part-time care – usually a half day for part or all of the week during school term-times. They will only be useful to working parents who work very short hours, unless they are supplemented with other care.

Playgroups

These provide supervised play for three to five year olds, and are often held in church halls or community centres that are also used for other activities. They usually offer half-day sessions (commonly just mornings) though extended day playgroups are being introduced in some areas, offering full day care and providing a meal. Playgroup leaders will have been on playgroup training courses organised by the Pre-school Playgroup Association (PPA). You will pay a small charge for each half day your child attends. Your local authority should have a list of local groups, or contact the PPA (see 'Addresses', page 215).

Nursery schools and classes

Some local education authorities offer free nursery education for three to five year olds, usually for half-days (9.30–12.00 or 1.00–3.30), but it may be possible for your child to stay for whole days, and rarely there may also be extended provision for working parents beyond 3.30 pm. The nursery may be attached to a primary school, and may be a good way of introducing your child to school in general, or to that particular school if you intend them to stay on there. Whether or not there is a nursery place available, fours and rising fives will start in a reception class. (A recent survey found that 90 per cent of four year olds attend reception classes.)

Private nursery schools and nursery departments attached to preparatory schools may offer half-day or full-day nursery education, again ending around 3.30 pm. They are expensive and holidays tend to be longer than those of state schools. Despite the high cost, there are often long waiting lists and in some places you need to apply for a place as soon as your child is born!

CHILDCARE FOR SCHOOL CHILDREN

It's easy to imagine that childcare will become much easier to organise once your children are at school. In fact, the opposite is often the case! School hours are far shorter than a usual working day, and school holidays much longer than yours are likely to be – unless you're a teacher! It can be difficult to bridge the gap between your needs and those of your children. You're likely to need a patchwork of care to fit around school times.

You may be able to adapt an existing carer to fit your new requirements; your childminder may be happy to have your child before or after school, and if she lives near to your chosen school she may also do the taking and picking up. If you have a nanny for a younger child, she will be able to do the same. But if this is your only child, or your youngest child, you probably won't have enough work to give her, and it seems extravagant to pay her for hours you don't need any more. One possibility is for her to find another family to work for who will agree to her having your child for out of school hours (see 'Sharing a nanny', page 127). Otherwise, you may need to find a new carer for the hours you need.

Family and friends may be a good solution for school age children (see page 114) or you may decide to employ an au-pair (see page 128). There are also out of school clubs that supervise children until parents can collect them. They provide a range of activities and fun in a relaxed atmosphere. Kids' Club Network was set up in 1981 to promote out of school care and play for over-fives. There are now more than a thousand clubs funded by government, Training and Enterprise Councils, employers and charitable trusts.

"I used to have to let the boys (aged seven and nine) walk home from school and take care of themselves till I got in around 5.30. Now I know they're safe and happy at the club until I can collect them."

John (34) car mechanic

For more information, contact Kids' Club Network (see 'Addresses', page 215).

As your children get older, they may come to resent having someone to look after them when you're at work, vehemently rejecting the idea of needing a 'babysitter' or taking an instant dislike to the person you organise to care for them, and if so can make life very difficult. You, on the other hand, may feel unhappy about allowing them to arrive home from school to an empty house or spend time in the holidays unsupervised. You may also be unwilling to give older children the responsibility of being in charge of younger brothers and sisters. If this is the case, you may be able to justify having a carer on their behalf. Depending on the age of your children, you could perhaps arrange for a neighbour to have them for a short while after school, or to be available if they need anything. Some parents find an au-pair works well with older children, being around if there's problem and perhaps preparing an evening meal (see page 129).

There actually isn't a legal age at which you may leave your children alone at home. As a parent, you are responsible for their well-being and should not leave them in a situation where they may come to harm. Only you can judge when you feel they are ready to take more responsibility for themselves. Try to avoid big confrontations, but be clear and firm about what you are and are not happy for your child to do, and check out regularly that the arrangements are working. If the children are at home alone, you may want to check up that they've arrived safely by telephoning from work.

"I was always worried about what Matthew would get up to during the school holidays while I was at work. I knew some of his friends were coming round to the house, smoking and goodness knows what while I was out. While there are holiday playschemes for younger children, there's very little provision for teenagers."

Anthea (36) travel agent

TRAINING AND QUALIFICATIONS

There are several different courses and qualifications relevant to the care of children of certain ages. You may feel more confident employing someone who's had relevant training, or you may attach more importance to experience, with younger brothers and sisters, perhaps, or with other families. Ideally, you will find someone with both, and will probably let your instinct guide you to some extent. It helps to know a little about what different training involves when deciding if you want to insist on it.

COUNCIL FOR AWARDS IN CHILDREN'S CARE AND EDUCATION (CACHE)

The Council for Awards in Children's Care and Education (CACHE) is the body formed in April 1994 from the merging of the Council for Early Years Awards (CEYA) and the National Nursery Examination Board (NNEB).

Someone with NNEB training will have done a two year full-time or three year part-time course, involving a combination of college work and short-term practical placements. Minimum requirements for the course are usually two GCSEs, but many students will have more. Students learn how children from birth to seven years grow and develop and how to look after them. Topics include physical care such as supporting breastfeeding mums, preparing and giving bottle feeds, bathing; health issues such as screening tests, immunisation and common ailments; how children learn and the importance of play; emotional development, including the importance of secure adult-child relationships; and social relationships, including changing patterns of family life.

Students also get practical experience with different age groups through placements in maternity units, day nurseries, nursery or infant classes, and in families.

OTHER COURSES AND QUALIFICATIONS

Courses may be organised by BTEC (Business and Technician Education Council), City and Guilds or NAMCW (National

Association for Maternal and Child Welfare) and run by many further education colleges. The new NVQs are a system of awards for people involved in vocational work, full or part time, waged or unwaged. There are a series of NVQs specifically designed for those working in childcare and education. Assessment takes place in the work setting rather than by examination. Private nursery training colleges such as Norland College offer courses from 18 months to three years, covering NNEB and additional qualifications. For a Norland Diploma, students are required to work for nine months as a probationary nursery nurse with a family once they have completed the course.

Qualifications such as the PPA (Pre-school Playgroups Association) Foundation Course, or a teacher training qualification are relevant to caring for children of certain ages. Montessori nursery training includes NNEB training, and promotes a child-centred approach that is useful in the home, playgroups or nursery classes. Children are guided and directed in a carefully planned and structured environment, with freedom of choice and expression.

Kids' Club Network offers courses on setting up and running out-of-school clubs (see page 141). For more information on training, contact CACHE (see 'Addresses' page 215).

THE CHILDREN'S ACT AND CHILDCARE

The Children's Act 1989 came into effect in 1991, and includes guidance and regulations about day-care provision, recommends good practice, and identifies the duties of local authorities to provide day-care themselves or facilitate its provision by others, including their role of providing advice, registration, inspection and review.

Compulsory registration aims to ensure standards of care for young children. Local authorities must keep a register of individual childminders or organisations (such as day nurseries, extended day or sessional playgroups, creches and private nursery schools) offering full-time, part-time or out of school care to one or more children under the age of eight. Anyone providing day care for payment, for more than two hours in any day, must register (apart from those who are exempt – see below), and if your carer was registered before the Children's Act came into effect, they will have to re-register. Your local authority register may be a good source of information about local childcare availability.

When assessing whether someone is 'fit' to look after children under eight, the local authority will consider their previous experience, relevant qualifications and training, their ability to provide warm and consistent care, physical health and mental stability, and any known involvement in criminal cases of child abuse. Others who live or work on the premises – for example your childminder's partner, or the caretaker at the nursery school – also have to be 'fit to be in the proximity of children under eight'.

Where babies are cared for, the local authority may require there to be a separate room for them, and staff rotas that allow as much continuity of care as possible, with each baby being cared for by one person during each shift. Carers may need to have NNEB, BTEC or other relevant training.

Premises also have to measure up to certain standards, including safety (fires, electric sockets, stairs, glass doors, smoke detectors, safe equipment, ponds fenced in etc.), washing and toilet facilities, facilities for rest and sleep, control of any pets present, and outside play areas. Desirable space for day nurseries is specified, and no room should have to accommodate more than 26 children.

The ratio of staff to children is recommended as:

- **For childminders:**
  Under five: three children to one minder
  Five to eight years: six children to one minder (with no more than three under five)
- **For day-care:**
  Under two: one carer to three children
  Two to three years: one carer to four children
  Three to five years: one carer to eight children
  Five to eight years: one carer to eight children

WHO'S EXEMPT FROM COMPULSORY REGISTRATION?

The following people do not need to register:

- **a relative** who cares for your child;
- **foster parents** and others with parental responsibility;
- **someone who cares for a child in the child's own home,** or works for two sets of parents and cares for the children in one of their homes.

Some establishments, such as schools, hospitals and children's homes are exempt. Also, occasional childcare, provided less than six days a year, for example a creche at a conference, need not be registered, but the organisers should still notify the local authority.

8 MAKING IT WORK

SETTLING YOUR CHILD

Whatever type of childcare you decide on, it's important to take time to help your child get used to new arrangements gradually so that he settles in happily. If you're going back to work for the first time since having children, or have had a break from work, the settling-in period may take longer, but even if your child is used to being left, a new childcare arrangement needs to be introduced gradually. How easily your child settles will depend on several things:

- **Have they ever been left with other people before** and was it a positive experience? Even if you haven't worked till now you may still have used babysitters or left your child with grandparents or other family members for short periods of time. (In fact, if you're planning to return to work, it's worth making sure both you and your child do get used to brief periods of separation beforehand.)
- **Are they going to be cared for at home** in familiar surroundings and with some favourite toys at hand, or will they be somewhere new with other children to get used to.
- **Are you leaving more than one child,** so that they will have each other as familiar playmates.
- **How old are they?** Newborn babies up to six months of age are likely to settle more easily than older babies or toddlers who may have reached a clingy phase and will not be able to understand when you say you're coming back.
- **How long and how often are you going to leave them?** Children seem to respond best to a routine, whatever it is. Younger

children may find it easier to be left for shorter times – several half days may be better than a few whole days, but of course this may not suit you so well or fit in with the demands of your work.

Some children seem to find new experiences easy, will quickly start relating to a new carer, and will be happy for you to leave without a backward glance. Don't be hurt! Your child is obviously feeling very secure. Others may take longer, and may need your support until a strange situation begins to feel more familiar. If your child is going to be cared for by someone in your own home, arrange some time when you can be there with them, doing things together and encouraging your child to get to know the new carer. This is also a chance to explain where things are kept, how different pieces of equipment work, and to go through your child's usual routine. If your child is being cared for somewhere else, stay with them for the first few visits, helping them to have a go with new toys, join in activities on offer and enjoy mealtimes. In either situation, you can gradually withdraw into the background, but still be around for a while if you're needed. You'll be able to judge when your child is ready for you to actually leave them. Play it by ear; you may want to go for short periods at first, building up to the full length of care over a day or two. Of course there may be tears, but having taken time to settle your child in, you can feel much more confident that these will quickly disappear. If you're worried, it's worth telephoning from work to find out how things are. Also, talk things through regularly with the person or people looking after your child to get a picture of how well your child has settled over time.

Very occasionally, children find it extra difficult to settle into a new routine. It's very distressing to be told that your child has been tearful or miserable for much of the time you've been away. You will need to decide how long you can let the situation continue, and may need to ask your employer for time to help settle your child again. Rather than change your childcare arrangement altogether, try staying with your child in their care situation again, getting them to take part in different activities that they particularly enjoy and gradually building up their confidence. If you are using group care, talk through the difficulties with staff and make sure your child can have one main carer and lots of individual attention until things improve.

You do need to also consider if the care your child is getting is right for him. Sometimes it is necessary to face the fact that it's not going to work out, and find a new arrangement.

"I knew Jonathan hadn't settled very well with his childminder. I'd only just gone back to work and wasn't sure what to expect, but my instinct told me that things weren't right. He was clingy when I left him there, and subdued when I collected him. I felt very stressed and couldn't concentrate on my work. Then my minder told me she was going through a lot of personal problems, and wouldn't be able to keep Jonathan on. The new minder was quite different – warm and loving and he settled in very quickly. Everything fell into place."

Sue (26) accounts clerk

If the situation above hadn't resolved itself, Jonathan's mum would have needed to talk through things with her childminder and perhaps spent some time there trying to settle Jonathan in and getting more insight into what was upsetting him.

With a childminder

Once you've chosen a childminder, you will need to introduce your child gradually. It's important to get to know your childminder and take time to talk with her about how things are going, and what your child has been up to. If you're both too tired at the end of a busy day, make a regular time to talk together, perhaps during an evening or over the weekend. Make sure you are punctual in picking your child up and paying your childminder – remember, this is their job and they probably rely on the income you provide.

With luck, once you've found a childminder they will be able to provide many years of reliable care – perhaps taking on a second child when it comes along, and keeping on an older child for shorter hours once she starts school.

"We've had five very happy years with our childminder, Marie. David went there when he was seven months old, and she now has my daughter, Amy, full-time, and David after school and in the holidays. Her own children are grown up, and because she's so experienced with children she's helped me through any difficult phases we've had with ours. I've been delighted they've had such consistency of care, too."
Sophie (31) education officer

With a nanny

Once you have found a new nanny, it's good to agree on a trial period of so many months, after which time you can both review things. In the early days you will want to spend some time helping her get used to your family and your ways, letting her see how you deal with different situations, and getting your child used to her. It may help to write down some of the key things she needs to know – for example, your child's daily routine, what he likes to eat and when, where things are kept, how to use the washing machine, where you and your partner can be contacted, and some emergency numbers such as your family doctor.

If your nanny is living in and this is the first time you've shared your home with someone, you need to give yourself and your partner time to adjust. Work out how much time you will share and how much privacy you wish to maintain. She may welcome the chance to share a meal with you, but then appreciate time to herself with her own TV or friends. Weekends may seem strange at first, but you will probably find she spends much of her free time out of the house if she is in most of the week with the children. Everyone finds their own way to deal with live-in help, but you'll probably find the more flexible you can all be, the more relaxed things will feel in the long run.

Whether or not your nanny lives in, you will want to make time to hear about what your child has been busy with, any little details about things they are learning to do, funny things they have said, or creative works of art they have brought home for you. You will need to talk through any problems that are concerning you or your nanny. You might also want to know in advance where your nanny is planning to go or do, so you can keep track of things. Communication is the key to making things run smoothly for your child.

CHANGING NEEDS

It's not possible to find a once-and-for-all solution to childcare. Your needs will change as babies grow into children, start playgroup or school, new children arrive, your work commitments change, or caring arrangements come to an end for different reasons. Much of it may be beyond your control. Not only may your main childcare needs change. As children get older and become involved in a variety of activities outside the home, you may need to enlist the help of friends or other parents to do some of the ferrying to and fro, especially if your carer cannot drive or is unwilling to do a lot of running around. These arrangements tend to change frequently. Just when you've found a parent to walk your son round to your childminder's after school each day, he announces he's joined the school chess club and will be staying late one night a week; or your daughter, who has been going with a friend to gymnastics, gets promoted to the next group and so can't get a lift home. No one thing is too disastrous, but taken together it means you are constantly juggling, arranging and rearranging.

Your needs may change from week to week. While a job offering school holidays may sound ideal, if you have pre-school children in full-time care during term time, you will need to cancel their care during the holidays. Childminders are usually flexible, and may charge only a retainer for the weeks you don't need them, providing they have plenty of notice. But if you use a day nursery or a nanny, they may find it harder to keep the place open for you unless you pay. The same issue may arise when you have another child and want to care for your first child yourself while you are at home on maternity leave. You may decide it is better not to disrupt the arrangement you have, especially if your child is happy and settled into a routine, and you're worried it will be difficult to find suitable alternative care. The downside of this is that you will have to pay for unnecessary care, and will not be able to spend the time with your child. Talk with your carer about your situation, and what you would like to do, and see if you can come to some agreement that suits you both.

Changing your childcare arrangements too often may be stressful not only for you but for your children too. Young children need to develop a bond with the person who cares for them day to day, and respond well to familiar routines. Too many changes can be unsettling, though of course sometimes this just cannot be avoided. If your child is old enough to understand it will help to prepare her well in advance of any changes. Explain why things are changing and what the new arrangement will be. Make sure she understands that she's not the cause of the changes; children often feel responsible and guilty for the things that happen in their life, and need to know that they haven't done anything wrong. If they've grown very close to their carer, you may want to keep in touch with them, and reassure your child that you are not going to disappear too. Even if things have not been good, it's best not to openly criticise the carer in front of your child – this may make them confused about their own feelings and anxious about the next person who takes charge of them.

"I was very happy with the childminder I used for Jennie. While I was on maternity leave I wanted to spend more time with her and also save on childcare fees. My minder couldn't afford to keep a vacancy open for me but luckily knew of someone who was looking for short-term care. When I went back to work, she found a place for the baby too."

Marilyn (33) trainer

"Maja continued to go to her childminder while I was on maternity leave. When I went back to work, she didn't have a place for the baby so I found someone else for him but using two different childminders got too difficult, and in the end I found yet another one who could take them both on. I got a reduction for having two children there, too."

Anne (25) office worker

CRISES AND CONTINGENCY PLANS

However good your childcare, and whatever careful arrangements you've made, there's always the possibility of a crisis.

WHEN YOUR CHILD IS ILL

It's what we all dread! You wake to find your child has a raging temperature or unexplained rash; or commute for an hour into work only to get a phone call almost at once saying your child has had an accident at school and could you collect her. Whatever the problem, when your child is ill your work is likely to be disrupted, at least for a while. Obviously, if your child is seriously ill or very unwell, they will need you and you will want to be with them. Most employers will allow you some leave to care for a sick child. If not, the only alternative may be to pretend you yourself are ill, although after three days you will need to produce a medical certificate. Even if there is no formal agreement at work, it's worth while talking to your boss or personnel department to see if you can have some time off, if necessary unpaid.

Once your child is over the worst or if she is only off-colour, you'll probably be able to leave her at home with someone. If you have a nanny or mother's help who comes to your home anyway, this won't be a problem. They should expect sometimes to have to look after an unwell child and will be quite competent to do so. You may feel less happy about leaving your child with an au-pair who perhaps lacks the experience to be able to cope well with a demanding or irritable child. If so, consider some of the contingency plans below. If you carer usually takes your other children to school or elsewhere you may need to arrange for someone else to take and fetch while your poorly child is too unwell to go out.

A childminder may be willing to cope with a child who's just a bit off-colour, although if she cares for other children too she may want to avoid them coming into contact with anything infectious or contagious. Group care like day nurseries, playgroups, nurseries and schools will not be able to cope with your child until she is fully recovered and feeling fit enough for the hurly burly again. If you send her back before she's ready for it, you may simply add to your problems by having to go and collect her again. These establishments are quick to telephone and ask you to collect a child who seems unwell and is struggling to get through the day.

WHEN YOUR CARER IS ILL

If your child is cared for by one main carer (a nanny, mother's help, au-pair or childminder), you'll need alternative help if they fall ill. Of course this isn't likely to happen very often – many mothers are amazed that over a number of years their carer never had a day off for illness – but it's best to be prepared. A live-in carer may be able to struggle on with a minor complaint, while someone who travels daily may not feel up to making the journey. For something more serious, find out how long they anticipate needing off, so that you can plan accordingly. If it's likely to be just a few days or a week, you may be able to find a friend or family member to help out. For longer, you may need to sort out other temporary cover. If it's treatment that they know of in advance – for example, some dental work or an operation – you will have more time to make alternative arrangements, which is easier than a sudden crisis.

"My childminder was so conscientious that she arranged for her wisdom teeth to be removed during our holiday, so we wouldn't be disrupted."

Caroline (35) nurse

WHEN YOU ARE ILL

You may think this wouldn't disrupt your childcare arrangements, but if you are the one who usually does the taking and fetching to childcare or school, then you may need help. If you have a partner, they may be able to take on more, or a friend or neighbour. If you have to go to hospital or are seriously ill at home, you'll obviously need a lot of support with all the hundred and one things you usually juggle.

WHEN CHILDCARE SUDDENLY FALLS THROUGH

When you've established good childcare and everything is going well, it can be very stressful to find out that it's going to end. Of course, people change jobs, move away, take up new commitments, and you will probably be faced with this situation at some point in your 'working parent' career. If your childcare stops with little notice then this will feel more like a crisis. When you take on someone as childcarer, you should agree what notice should be given on either side when the arrangement ends. Usually this will be four weeks, or less if this suits you both, and will give you a breathing space to find new childcare. But sometimes people leave with very little notice, leaving you with a crisis.

"My nanny sat me down and said she'd been offered a job in a nursery, and was taking a holiday before she started. I couldn't believe it when she said she wouldn't be coming next day! Worse still, she didn't even say goodbye properly to my daughters who were two and four at the time and whom she'd looked after part-time for the past year."

Danielle (30) antique dealer

"The au-pair gave me no warning at all. She just announced one night that she'd booked a ticket home because she missed her boyfriend. I panicked completely because I had a really busy period at work, and finding a new girl and settling her in was going to take a lot of time and energy I just couldn't spare."

Janet (32) civil engineer

ADDITIONAL WORK COMMITMENTS

Everything may go smoothly until you get asked to take on more at work, or perhaps have to stay away from home for a conference or business meeting. If this means your usual childcare won't provide the cover you need, then you may need to put your contingency plans into action.

CONTINGENCY PLANS

It helps to have some contingency plans in place for any sudden crisis that may occur to affect your usual childcare. You'll feel more in control and less stressed if you have at least some idea about where you might turn for help. The longer you have lived in an area, the bigger your network of local friends and contacts is likely to be, so the more people you may be able to call on for help. Work permitting, you may be able to reciprocate with a friend when they need a favour. This way you won't feel so awkward about asking.

The more children you have, the harder you may find it to arrange emergency cover for them. On the other hand, if you have more than one carer involved in looking after your children at different times, then if one is unable to do it, the other may be able to fill the gap for a while.

"Sarah usually goes to my mum's house two mornings a week, and to Shirley, my childminder, the other three mornings. When mum was ill, Shirley offered to have her every day, so Sarah really wasn't affected at all."

Claudia (23) receptionist

"I needed someone to take and pick up Alex from school while Sophie was ill with mumps and not well enough to go out in the cold, so the nanny had to stay in with her. My neighbour was willing to do it for me as her daughter goes to a school nearby."

Julia (34) lecturer

Here are some possibilities for contingency plans:

- Your social services department will keep a register of local childminders (see page 144) and may be able to put you in touch with one who has a vacancy and is willing to take on your child on a temporary basis.

CHILDCARE AT A GLANCE

Quality of care	Family & friends	Childminder	Mother's help	Nanny	Au-pair	Day nursery	Workplace nursery/creche	Playgroup or nursery class
One main carer who child attaches to	• Yes	• Yes	• Yes (supplements you)	• Yes	• Yes, but less intensive care	• No, but could be keyworker		• One main leader plus volunteers/assistants
Continuity of care	• Probably, providing arrangement works out	• Likely to offer long-term care	• Likely to move on quite soon	• Varies from person to person	• Turnover high	• Staff turnover may be high depending on way workers are treated		• Likely
Other children cared for alongside	• Family: usually no – Friends: often their own children too	• Usually yes – ages mixed	• Only your own	• Usually only your own, or may share with another family	• No	• Yes: large group, mixed age	• Yes: large group, mixed age	• Yes: large group, similar age
Educational activities as well as care	• Possibly	• Possibly	• Possibly	• Possibly	• Unlikely	• Probably	• Probably	• Yes: a main focus
Trained and experienced	• Usually experience only	• Usually experience only	• Little	• Usually trained, experience varies	• No	• Proportion of staff are trained		• Usually trained and experienced
Must be registered with local authority	• No	• Yes	• No	• No	• No	• Yes	• Yes	• Yes
Convenience Have to get child up and out in morning	• Possibly	• Yes	• No	• No	• No	• Yes	• Yes	• Yes
Punctuality at end of day important	• Possibly	• Yes	• Less so if they live in	• Less so if they live in	• Less so	• Yes	• Yes	• Yes
Help in your home	• Possibly	• No	• Housework: washing, ironing, etc.	• Child-related home duties	• Housework: washing, ironing, etc.	• No	• No	• No
Hours shorter than usual working day – will need supplementing	• No	• No	• No	• No	• Yes, for pre-school children	• No	• No	• Yes

Problems when your child is ill	• Possibly	• Probably, if she cares for other children	• Possibly inexperienced to look after	• No	• Inexperienced and hours too short	• Yes	• Yes	• Yes
Problems when your carer is ill	• Yes	• Yes	• Yes	• Yes	• May be able to cope with minor illness	• No	• No	• No
Problems when you are ill	• Probably not	• Getting child there	• No	• No	• No	• Getting child there • Will need help outside their hours		
Second child may be cared for at some time	• Possibly, including school children	• Possibly, including school children	• Yes, including school children	• Yes, including school children	• Yes, including school children	• Possibly, if pre-school age	• Possibly, if pre-school age	• Possibly, if pre-school age
Holidays	• May be able to arrange holidays to coincide with yours					• Open all year round	• May have fixed holidays, eg university holidays	• Open during school term times
Geared to your own needs *Child may be taken to activities, groups*	• Yes	• Possibly	• Yes	• Yes	• Yes	• No	• No	• No
You can specify how you want things done, meals etc.	• Possibly	• Less so	• Yes	• Yes	• Yes	• Less so	• Less so	• Less so
Flexible hours to suit your particular needs	• Possibly	• Possibly	• Yes	• Yes	• Yes (up to 5 hours a day – may need to avoid college hours)	• No	• No	• No
Cost	• Low cost or pay in kind	• £50–90 a week (fees/salaries vary depending on location and experience)	• £80–100 per week net	• £90–130 per week net	• Around £35 per week + board and lodging	• May be subsidised or free to high-need families	• May be subsidised	• Depends if public or private sector
Age groups cared for	• All	• All	• Usually 0–5 with help	• 0–5, possibly school child too	• Best from 5 years up	• 6 months–5 years	• 6 months–5 years	• 3 plus

- Your workplace nursery may be able to accommodate an older child after school if your usual care arrangement for her has broken down temporarily.
- Sometimes an employer is flexible about you taking a child into work with you, or you working from home on a short-term basis.
- Your partner may be able to help out more than usual, and cover some of your gaps.
- You could use an agency to find you temporary or urgent help. They may have girls on their books who are available for work straightaway, and will have checked out their references and experience. You will probably have to pay quite a large fee.
- You may have friends with childminders or nannies who would be willing to take your child on temporarily. Obviously you will have to pay them.
- Could someone in your family help out on a day-to-day basis, or come and stay with you till things return to normal?
- Could you ask a friend or neighbour to help out with looking after your child at her house, coming to your house, taking and delivering from day-care or school?
- Could a friend have your child to stay overnight to help you out? Or could your child stay with a school friend – you could offer to reciprocate another time.
- The parents of your children's friends at school may be able to help out before or after school on a temporary basis, and your child will settle easily if he knows the family well.

9 COPING WITH CHANGE

Holding down a job and raising children is a constant balancing act and sooner or later something can crop up which may alter everything. Change is a natural part of all our lives and while it can sometimes be foreseen and planned for. Things may also happen unexpectedly and you can find yourself faced with a sudden crisis which demands an immediate solution.

You may be asked to work late, your carer or your child may fall ill – your carer may leave with next to no notice. Contingency plans to tackle crises relating to childcare arrangements are discussed in detail on page 157. This chapter looks at some of the other more far-reaching changes which could happen, on either the home or the work front.

CHANGES IN THE FAMILY

A SECOND BABY

If you are thinking about having another baby there are a number of factors you might want to consider, not least whether you really want one.

You shouldn't feel pressured into having more because other people think it is 'better'. People sometimes argue that only children may be spoiled or lonely, but recognising the possible pitfalls is the first step towards taking steps to avoid them. You can be careful not to over-indulge a child because she is an 'only', you can encourage her to make friends and ensure she has a social life of her own. Having another baby simply to keep the first child company may seem a good idea but, as anyone who has had to deal with squabbling children and sibling rivalry will tell you, things don't always work out the way you imagine.

You may feel that having another baby might make the balancing act between home and work even more difficult, if not impossible. Or you may feel that now you are a more experienced parent, everything will be easier second time around. As always, when making important decisions, it is essential to sit down and work through the pros and cons of all the options, and then decide to do what feels right for you.

Once you've decided that you would like another baby, it would be sensible to consider the question of timing – even if family planning is not yet an exact science!

Ask yourself whether you want to get the 'having babies' phase of your life over in one go, or would you rather see the first through toddlerhood before the next is born?

Some parents say that having children close together was worth the hard work at the time. One of the main advantages of a small age gap is that children can keep each other company as they grow older. And, for working parents, the other is that the children have roughly the same childcare needs at roughly the same time.

"I never planned to have two children only 15 months apart and the first few years were exhausting. But once they were both out of nappies and able to feed themselves, life got better and it's been great since. They fall out from time to time, but in general they are the best of friends – and half the trouble as a result."

Caroline (38) quality controller

Some parents prefer to wait two to three years, or longer, before having another baby. Waiting gives women time to recover from the physical demands of pregnancy, birth and breastfeeding. It gives parents time to settle the first child into a pattern of sleeping at night – or at least, going to bed at a regular time. It gives the first child time to be babied and then steered through the toddler years before a new baby is born.

On the other hand, this kind of age gap never really closes up. The two children may become friends and playmates, but until they are both grown-up there will always be a difference between a baby and a child, a child and a teenager, a teenager and an adult.

Thinking about the following list of questions, which address some of the practical issues involved, may also help you make up your mind.

- Will you (or your partner) be able to cope with work, pregnancy and a clingy toddler who still needs lifting and carrying?
- How much sleep will you get with a newborn and a toddler who may still wake up at night?
- Will you need to buy more baby equipment: a double buggy, another cot, double the number of nappies?
- Will your carer take on another baby/child, or will you need to rethink your childcare plans?
- If you space your children out, you will need childcare for longer: would it be more economical to fit them in to a shorter timescale?
- Would you have to change your work arrangements (go part-time, take a career break etc.) in order to handle the demands of having another child now?
- Do you want to change your work-pattern, and would this be a good time to do it?
- How will having another child affect your financial security: will you have less money coming in for a while?

You need to talk through all these issues together. But no matter when you decide to go ahead, you will need to anticipate how pregnancy and a second child will alter the existing balance between work, home, you and the family.

Working through a second pregnancy may be easier in some respects than working through a first, if only because the changes that take place within your body have a certain familiarity. You may still suffer from the same problems, like morning sickness, but by this time you are more likely to have worked out the best ways to cope. (If not, see pages 15–33)

On the other hand a second pregnancy can be very different from a first and you can't assume that you will automatically sail through it, just because you did before.

Nor can you make any assumptions about the way other people will react. Some women say that people they work with are less than pleased to hear about plans for a second maternity leave, particularly if it comes hard on the heels of the first. And while some find that partners are more willing to share the burden at home – particularly when it comes to looking after the first child – others may find it hard to get the extra help and support they need.

Dealing with difficulties like these may feel harder since you are quite likely to feel more tired than you did first time round. After all, on top of everything else, this time you also have a child to look after.

For some parents planning to have a second child can also be the time to rethink the balance between parenting and work. You may already have been considering a switch to part-time working or stopping work altogether for a while. Your partner, if you have one, may be at a stage in his working life where he wants to invest more time and energy in his family than his job – or he may be working harder than ever. Whatever your situation, now is a good time to take stock.

If your employer is still the same one as during your last pregnancy you will already know how family-friendly the organisation is. This may well have some bearing on what you decide to do next.

Childcare arrangements

Whether you are planning to carry on as before or not, having a second child almost certainly means rethinking your childcare arrangements. Whether you rely on help from family or friends, send your child to a minder or a nursery, or employ a nanny, mother's help or au-pair, you can't assume that another baby will be welcomed with open arms.

If you are going to have to make different arrangements, these should ideally be done well in advance so that your first child has plenty of time to adjust. That means talking to your existing carer during your pregnancy, to sound them out about looking after the new baby, too. Things may depend on the age of your first child – whether they are about to start school, for instance.

If your carer is interested in the possibility you will also have to work out how much extra you will end up paying and what you will do in the period when you are on maternity leave. A carer may agree to keep a place open if you want your first child at home more, but may expect you to pay for the place.

When it comes to the second child, a childminder may offer a reduced rate. A nanny might agree to look after the new baby, but she might also feel a wage increase only reasonable to reflect the increased responsibility and workload. You might save money by looking for a new nanny hired to care for two, but would the upset to you and your first child be worth it?

If you can arrange it, there are several of advantages in keeping the same care arrangements going throughout your pregnancy and after your second child arrives:

- your first child has continuity of care;
- your second child will get to know the carer from a very early stage;
- when you start your maternity leave you will get some time to rest and relax if your child is still being cared for by someone else;
- when you go into labour, it may be possible for your carer to look after your first child;
- you will have some time alone with the baby after the birth.

A second baby checklist

- Do I/we plan a change to our working arrangements which will have a knock-on effect on child-care?
- Will my/our current carer/s take on the new addition too?
- How much extra would this cost?
- What else is available/practicable?
- Would a new arrangement suit us practically and/or financially?
- How much upheaval would a change cause to my child/me/ the rest of the family?

If you do decide to have another baby

- Make sure you know you know what rights and benefits you are entitled to (see page 60). These do change from time to time, so don't assume everything will be the same as it was before.
- Book in for a refresher course of antenatal classes. Ask your midwife about these, or contact the NCT. The NCT classes,

for instance, may deal with the practicalities of having more than one child.

- If you have a partner, encourage him to look after your first child when you are both at home. Not only will this give you a much-needed rest, but it will stand you all in good stead once your attention is taken up with the baby.
- See if you can give yourself time to unwind after finishing work. Would your child-minder agree to give your child tea so you could go home and have a quiet bath on your own before picking her up an hour later than usual – if not every day, then perhaps once or twice a week?
- Find quiet activities you can do with your child so you can rest while he plays. Anything that can be done while you sit or lie down is worth a try: crayoning, jigsaw puzzles, imaginary games like doctors and nurses (with you as the patient), looking at picture books, listening to story tapes. If you have a video, you could record some of the children's TV programmes during the day to watch together in the evening.
- Could you turn bath-time into a longer water-play session? Give your toddler empty yoghurt pots, straws, toys that won't be hurt by being immersed in water and let her play while you sit and watch her. If you are not too huge you could always get in yourself.

"When I was expecting my second baby I started a Treasure Box. It contained just junk, really, but the kind of junk that amuses two-year-olds. Empty egg boxes, cotton reels and a ribbon for threading. Bubble cellophane that could be popped and old Christmas cards. When I needed to put my feet up before the baby arrived – and when I needed some time with him afterwards – I used to tell the toddler she could have the Treasure Box. It worked a treat."

Kerry (28) dietician.

FROM TWO PARENTS TO ONE

Of all the life changes people have to deal with, losing a partner is one of the most traumatic, whether the loss is a result of divorce or bereavement.

Losing someone you loved – even if, in the case of a break-up, you no longer love them – is always difficult and is even more so where children are involved.

The end of a relationship is not only emotionally distressing, it brings changes all round; it involves questions such as where you live or how much money you have to live on. Divorce means sorting out who has day-to-day control of the children or who only sees them from time to time.

Breaking up can mean that you need to go out to work to bring in more money or it can mean giving up work because the cost of childcare has become prohibitive, or because the load which once was shared is too much to shoulder alone.

Bereavement also turns your life upside down. You will be grieving not just for the loss of someone you loved, but for the loss of your own identity as that person's partner and for the loss of a future you might have had together. At the same time you will be grappling with a range of feelings – including, perhaps, anger or despair at being left to handle everything alone.

This kind of reaction is perfectly normal. It is only human to experience a series of powerful emotional upheavals. These include shock, disbelief or denial, sadness and depression, guilt and anger.

Grieving isn't a tidy process. You won't necessarily work from one emotion to the next until you come out feeling better at the end. That said, provided you allow yourself to mourn your losses and you avoid getting stuck in a particular stage – guilt, say, or anger – you will, in time, be able to move on instead of looking back.

You may need help to do this. Other family members or friends may be willing listeners if you need to talk. *The Relate Guide to Starting Again* is a useful book to read. Or you might want to talk to a counsellor in person. A few companies offer their staff counselling services, but these are few and far between. However, Relate sees individuals as well as couples. You can find the number of your nearest branch in the phone book. Or you could contact the British Association for Counselling for details of services in your area.

It is also important to recognise that your children will need help to cope with the changes. Most children would rather stay living with both parents, no matter how unhappy the relationship between them. They prefer the security of a familiar situation to the insecurity of the unknown.

The National Family Conciliation Council offers help to couples going through divorce or separation. Trained conciliators work with parents to help them reduce conflict and come to agreements, especially where children are concerned.

This checklist may help children cope with the situation.

- Reassure them that you still love them and this isn't their fault.
- Give them as much information as you can about what is going to happen: where they will live, go to school; where you will live; where their other parent will live; if you plan to carry on working/go back to work. If you can, reassure them that the daily routine will remain much the same.
- However upset or busy you are, don't expect the children to fill the gaps your partner used to. Of course older ones should

help around the house, but it may be better if you sat down with them and let them volunteer to do certain chores.

- Allow the children to express their feelings rather than trying to distract them from what they feel.
- Answer questions as honestly as you can.
- In the case of a divorce, no matter how hurt or bitter you feel, remember that children need to be allowed to love both parents.
- In the case of a bereavement, do share your feelings and memories.
- Be aware that the children may need more of your time than usual. This can be difficult if you are working and you may need to let other things, such as housework, slip for a while
- Try to ensure you are around at bedtime – that's when fears and deep feelings often surface.

If you are trying to hold down a job, run a home, look after children, cope with your feelings and deal with whatever has to be done after death or during divorce, it is understandable to feel under a great deal of strain.

Some people say that they found it hard to work when they were facing a future on their own. Others say that having a job was one of the few things which kept them on course, helped give them a new sense of identity, boosted their self-esteem or took their mind off their feelings.

"When my marriage broke up it was a real emotional upheaval, even though I was the one who decided we couldn't go on the way we were. I couldn't have given up my job then, as we certainly needed the money, but in many ways it was a relief to have part of my life carrying on as normal. It gave me a focus and a feeling that I could, at least, do something right."

Lyn (46) teacher

You may feel you need some time off. You may have to take some holiday time or compassionate leave. Some companies offer their employees family leave, usually between three and ten days a year, to cover domestic crises. If you are unable to cope, do see your GP. You may be able to go off sick for a while.

In any case, it is probably better not to make any hasty decisions about leaving your job or changing your work patterns until you have thought more carefully about the future. You will have to take your new financial situation into account. You may have to move house. You may have to think about changing your childcare arrangements because they no longer work, perhaps you no longer live near enough to the nursery, or you can't take your child to the childminder as your partner used to.

You need to take time to work all this through. The sections elsewhere in the book dealing with lone parents, childcare and returning to work will help you do so.

However, counsellors often advise that it is best not to make any major decisions, if you can avoid it, for the first six months to a year, until your emotions start to get back on an even keel. It may not be possible to wait that long, or you may find it difficult to reach any decisions at all, especially if you are not used to making them without consulting your partner.

The problems facing you may seem overwhelming if you look at them as one big obstacle. It can help to break down problems into individual tasks which can be tackled step by step.

- **What is the problem?** Identify the problem in detail and pinpoint what needs to be solved. e.g. *I have to earn more money but I don't know who would look after the children after school if I worked more hours.*
- **What is my goal?** Identify what you need to eliminate the

problem. e.g. *I need a better-paid job and to be sure the children are all right.*

- **How could I solve the problem?** Think of all the different ways you could achieve your goal. e.g. *Look for a better paid part-time job so you could still collect the children yourself; Look for a full-time job and pay another parent to collect the children after school and give them tea.*

- **What are the advantages and disadvantages of all the solutions?** Find out more about the possibilities and then compare them. e.g. *Part-time jobs are available. The money wouldn't be much more than I get now, but I'd feel happier if I was there to meet the children; I'd earn more if I worked full-time but I'd have to pay for childcare.*

- **Have I overlooked anything?** Check through your lists to see if there is anything you might have left out or need to know more about. e.g. *What jobs are available at the moment? How much do they actually pay? Would my current employer upgrade me or offer me more hours.*

- **Follow up by getting the information you need.** e.g. *There are both part-time and full-time jobs being advertised. After deductions for tax and insurance and the cost of childcare I'd be marginally better off working full-time than part-time. My current employer could offer me a full-time position if I was interested.*

- **Make an informed choice.** e.g. *I don't want to work full-time. I will look for a part-time job which pays better than my present one as this will bring in the extra money I need and allow me to look after the children myself.*

- **Set the wheels in motion.** e.g. *Visit employment agencies or check the ads in the local paper for part-time jobs.*

CHANGES IN DIRECTION

GOING BACK AFTER A LONG BREAK

Many women who have given up work to look after their children reach a point where they feel they would like to go back. Often they are not sure how to go about it. They may also be held back by a feeling that they might not be up to it. They might feel daunted by all the technological changes that have taken place while they have been concentrating on parenting. They might simply lack the confidence to go back and deal on equal terms with others who have not spent years at home.

If you are thinking about returning to work after a long break the first thing you should do is identify your goals. Ask yourself what you want and why you want it.

- Do you want to work for yourself, make lots of money, do something to help others, develop new skills, have a career?
- Do you want money to pay the bills, money to call your own, money for extras?
- Do you want a job so you can have some independence or simply something to do that gets you out of the house?
- Do you want a challenge, a chance to use your brain, or something that won't be too demanding but will enable you to meet other adults and talk about something other than husbands and children?

Once you have a rough idea of why you want to go back to work, you can begin to build up your confidence and take the first steps towards your goal.

You can begin by listing all your skills and achievements. This way you not only raise your own self-esteem by reminding yourself of all the things you do well, but you can begin to pinpoint the areas where you may need to take action before you start your job search.

The chart below will give you an idea of how you could go about it.

Communication skills	
College	Essays, reports, surveys.
Voluntary	Letter writing, co-ordinating, organising fund-raising, arranging transport, driven minibus.
Business	Word processing (own computer at home) at ease on telephone, can use fax and copiers.
Domestic	Time management, dealing with household accounts, budgeting.
People skills	
Family	Good at explaining homework, problem solving, mediating.
Voluntary	Co-ordinating, negotiating, making new contacts.
Creative skills	
Domestic	Decorating, gardening.
Voluntary	Ideas, thought up fund-raising schemes.

It may seem strange at first to think of all the things you do at home in this light, giving them as much prominence as the skills you acquired during your education and when you were employed. But they are just as important, and when it comes to looking for a job you should not be afraid to mention them. In fact, transferable skills like these are often what employers are looking for – so don't underestimate your capabilities or undervalue yourself.

Before you start looking for work

- There are courses for women on confidence building and assertiveness. Check with your local college for day or evening classes, or ask if your library has any information.
- If you want to get your brain in gear, join an organisation like the National Women's Register. Members meet in each others homes for evenings of debate and discussion with topics ranging from the serious to the more frivolous.
- Consider bridging the gap between home and work by taking on some voluntary work. If you return to work you will have to reorganise your home life, so this can be one way of finding out what works best for you. It is also a good way of building up your skills. The library will have information about local organisations. There may also be a local volunteer bureau listed in your phone book.
- Decide whether any of your skills need updating and find out how you might go about doing this.

You might find what you are looking for on your doorstep. Local colleges may offer return to study or Access courses, or courses designed specially for returners. Jobcentres can also provide information about training schemes, including those sponsored by TECs, local training and enterprise councils (LECs in Scotland), which are specifically aimed at women returners. It is also worth scanning the local papers, as courses are often advertised.

Distance learning is another option. The Open University runs a wide range of courses. Other avenues to explore include the

Open College and the National Extension College. (See 'Addresses' on page 216).

"I wanted to stay at home when my children were small but I didn't really know where to start looking for a job again once they were both at school. I saw a New Horizons course advertised in the local paper which seemed ideal as it aimed to get you ready to go back into the world of work. I really enjoyed it, it got my little grey cells working again, and it gave me the confidence to apply for my current job."

Janice (35) school secretary

One particularly useful source of advice and information will be the Women Returners Network (LWRN) which can let you know about courses on self-assessment, career planning or which can help to update you in your field. LWRN also produces *Returning to Work: A Directory of Education and Training for Women* which may be available in your library.

Parents At Work publishes a *Returner's Handbook* and runs one-day workshops called Back to Work.

Finding all the information you need may take some time. But make this process part of an overall plan. List the steps you need to take to reach your goal – getting a job. Then break big steps down into smaller stages, but give yourself a timescale so that you know what you should have done by when. Each time you can cross off a stage you will feel a sense of satisfaction at being closer to your goal.

One of your tasks will be to track down jobs you would like to apply for. You could start informally by contacting anyone you have met, either recently or in the past, who might be in a position to help. You don't have to ask for a job, but a simple request for information about what's going on in their field will let them know you are back in the market for work.

You may want to contact a network set up for women in a particular field: examples include Women in Management or Women in Banking. A full list can be obtained from the Women's National Commission.

Employers advertise in local and national newspapers as well as the trade press, or you may find something suitable on offer through an employment agency or a jobcentre.

Not all jobs are advertised: you might consider using a directory or Yellow Pages to contact employers in the field you want to work in, asking to be considered for any vacancies which might exist, either now or in the future.

If you are not used to writing letters, or if you are not sure what to say, get help. Your local jobcentre will be able to tell you if there is a job club which you could join. Not only is this one way of getting advice on how to approach employers, draw up a CV (see below) and handle interviews, but it can make you feel less isolated and more confident.

Some people make the mistake of drawing up a standard CV and sending it out with every job application. It is better to tailor a new CV each time, emphasising different aspects of your experience as appropriate, to show that you understand the needs of the job. If a job advertisement says 'languages would be an advantage', you might, for example, include spare-time activities where you have used foreign languages, as well as any educational qualifications.

Basic information should always include your name, address, telephone number, education, training, work history and references. You may also want to give your date of birth and marital status. Spare time activities and interests can be used to illustrate your skills or experience.

It is also important to present the gap in employment in a positive way. Think about the skills you acquired during your time at home and how these might relate to the job you are applying for. Managing on a tight budget might have taught you about financial planning. Running fund-raising events may have honed your organisational abilities.

Once you start working....

Of course, when you find yourself in the happy position of landing a job you wanted, you may assume that all your problems are over. In reality they are probably just starting! If your family has been used to having you at home full-time, it may take a while to adapt to the change. Advice on how to minimise the upheaval is given on page 107, 'When you first go back'.

CHANGING COURSE

If you are thinking of changing jobs or embarking on a new career then much of the advice about going back to work after a long break will apply (see above). You will need to ask yourself why you want a change, what you hope to get out of it and what the impact is likely to be on your life at home. You may need to acquire new skills or upgrade your existing ones. You will have to find an opening and convince an employer that you are what they are looking for.

On the other hand, instead of thinking about a change of job, you might be thinking about a change of workplace. More than two million people were working from home in 1992 and the forecasts predicted that the numbers would rise to more than four million by the mid 1990s.

One of the reasons for this, of course, is the growth in new technology – computers, faxes, modems and the like. Not only can you set up your own business at home, or work on a freelance basis, but you can be employed as a teleworker and communicate with your office electronically, rather than physically commuting every day.

Working from home has its attractions. No time wasted travelling. No time wasted fielding other people's phone calls. More time, in theory for your family. On the downside, working from home can feel very lonely and you need to be quite motivated and disciplined.

Would working from home suit you?

- Does your job have to be carried out in a certain place?
- Do you work better when you are supervised?
- Are most of your friends work colleagues?
- Do you solve work problems by talking them over with colleagues?
- Do you use your travelling time as a way to make the change from the working you and the home you?
- Do you prefer to work as part of a team?
- Do you prefer getting on with work without other people interfering?
- Do you have space to work from home?
- Do you like your own company?
- Do you hate commuting to work?
- Can you motivate yourself or do you prefer following instructions?
- Do you hate working surrounded by noise?

If you answered 'no' to the first five questions and 'yes' to the last, then you probably could work from home very successfully. Even if your answers were different, thinking about the issues raised by the questions should help you make up your mind.

In any case, before you make any changes, you should think more deeply about some of the practicalities involved.

- **where will you work?** Some people who work from home say the ideal situation is having somewhere to work where
  - you don't have to clear everything away at the end of each day
  - you can shut the door for peace and quiet
  - you won't be reminded about work still to be done when you are meant to be enjoying time with the family.

  Others manage to work on a corner of the kitchen table, or in their bedroom, and some say they enjoy having their family around them.

- **what hours will you work?** Are you planning to work a standard nine-to-five or will you start earlier, finish later, skip lunch-hours or something different, and how will this fit in with the your family commitments?

- **how much child-care will you need?** If your children are still young you won't be able to work and look after them at the same time – or, at least, not properly and not on a regular basis. (One of the advantages of working at home is that you are more likely to be able to juggle things in a crisis, if your child is off sick from school, for example.) Even if they are old enough to be going to school, the school day is much shorter than the average working day – and you may also need some kind of help during the holidays.

If you decide that working from home is what you want to do, then it is a good idea to establish some ground rules right from the start. Having rules will help everyone adjust to the idea that just because you are at home, you are not automatically available to do whatever it is they want you to.

For example, you may find yourself being asked to carry out

errands, take back library books, pick up dry cleaning, post letters. If you don't want to interrupt your work for these kind of tasks you will have to be firm. Explain that your work is important and that during your working hours it has to come first.

If your children are being cared for in the home you will also need to talk to your carer about the division of responsibility. You need to consider your carer's point of view: she won't find it easy if you rush to investigate every time you hear a child grizzling. And you probably won't appreciate it if she interrupts you all the time to ask about things she would have dealt with perfectly well by herself if you weren't there.

Depending on the age of your children, you may be able to explain to them that there will be times when your carer is 'on duty', and there will times when you are. Younger children are less likely to be able to grasp this idea and it may be easier all round if, when you are working, you keep out of sight as much as possible.

You will need to establish ground rules, too, about your work equipment. Try to make it clear that all your working materials are out of bounds. Of course with very young children you will just have to make sure that nothing is left around where they might be tempted to scribble on it or play with it.

If you use the telephone for work you will either have to ban children from answering it during your working hours or teach them to answer correctly and politely. The same applies to nannies, mother's helps and au-pairs. You may also have to tell others in the house (especially teenagers) that they may use the phone only when you are not working.

10 WORK ISSUES FOR LONE PARENTS

The challenges facing lone parents who work are the same as those which all working parents have to cope with only they're even more challenging! The physical and emotional demands of parenting may sometimes clash with work, and, coping single-handed makes this more likely. It's true that even in families with two parents who both work, the responsibility for looking after the children and home and organising childcare often rests mainly with one parent, most likely the mother. Some women bringing up children alone actually feel less hassled and more in control than they did when they lived with a partner and had them to look after too! But on the whole, it does help to have a partner who will share some of the jobs, take over to give you some space or cover in emergencies, and perhaps most important, who can give you emotional support. Lone parents have to look elsewhere for this. This chapter considers some of the particular challenges facing lone parents who work, and possible ways round them.

TAKING THE STRAIN

When you're on your own bringing up a child, there's no one to share the responsibilities and chores, so you're left with less time for your children, work, household tasks, and, most likely of all, yourself. It may often feel like there aren't enough hours in the day and you're more likely to be physically and emotionally drained and over-stretched. Responsibility for your children goes on 24 hours a day – it doesn't end when you hand them over to someone else and go off to work. When there's a crisis such as illness, or a burst boiler at school, it will be down to you to find a way round it, and there's only you to plan and keep one step ahead of the next problem.

So how do lone parents manage to cope with the double responsibility of children and work? There are certainly several benefits to be gained from having a job, besides the obvious one of an income, and for lone parents these may be especially compelling. In fact, many lone parents choose to work despite being only marginally better off financially once benefits have been adjusted. Having some kind of structure to your week and social contact with other adults may be an important consideration when you're living on your own with children. Part-time work may be especially helpful as it allows you to spend enough time with the children to avoid some of the guilt, and more time for all the other hundred and one tasks involved in running a home without overstretching you so much. The downside is that you'll earn less, and many lone parents don't have the luxury of choosing that option.

"I went back to work soon after David and I split up. The children took a while to adjust – they'd been used to having me around all the time, and resented going to the childminder after school at first. But because it made me feel so much better to get out and meet people and have a new interest, they soon saw the benefits – I wasn't so tense and down all the time – and came to accept it."

Margaret (35) secretary

MONEY MATTERS

One of the most pressing worries for many lone parents is money. A large proportion of all families with children are hard up, and this is especially likely for lone parent families. Only four in ten lone parents are employed, half in part-time work, and the UK has the third lowest employment rate for lone mothers in the EC. With more than 90 per cent of lone parents being women, who anyway earn less on average than men, it's not hard to see why many lone parent families are struggling to make ends meet. One study found that lone mothers earn on average 60 per cent of the average male wage. The way in which earned income and benefit payments interact means you may not be much better off unless you can take on a full-time job. The traditional nine-to-five working day does not fit in well with the shorter hours of play-school, nursery or school, so that even when your child is old enough for these you will need to organise childcare at the beginning or end of their day as well as during long holidays, and will not have a partner to share some of this with.

IS IT WORTH YOUR WHILE TO WORK?

As a lone parent, your three most likely sources of income, unless you have private savings or investments, are earned income, maintenance payments (if you've been married), and state benefits. The way in which these interact in the UK may mean that it is not financially worthwhile working, because of the knock-on effect of your wage on benefit payments. As your earnings rise, your income will increase by only a small proportion of this because means-tested benefits will be reduced, and you may become liable to pay income tax and national insurance contributions. In contrast to the situation here, many other EC countries have measures which empower lone parents in the labour market and thus reduce their dependency on the state.

A new earnings offset for childcare, introduced in October 1994, aims to help make it more worthwhile for parents to work by offsetting childcare costs up to a maximum of £40 per week when calculating entitlement to family credit. (For more about how this works, see 'Family credit', page 186).

So what are the different benefits and payments available, and how do they interact with each other and with any income which you earn or receive from elsewhere?

- **One parent benefit.** This benefit is for all lone parents with dependent children (under 16, or up to 18 in full-time education) except those receiving widow's benefit. It is not means-tested and not subject to income tax, but is taken into account in calculating some means-tested benefits. Since April 1993 it has been £6.05 per week.
- **Child benefit.** This is a universal benefit for all dependent children, paid to their main carer. It is not means-tested and not taxable, but it is taken into account in calculating some means-tested benefits.
- **Income support.** This is a means-tested benefit for people who are out of work or on very low incomes. As a lone parent you are eligible if you have dependent children (see 'one parent benefit' above), are not employed or work less than 16 hours a week. Child benefit, one parent benefit and maintenance payments are counted as income in calculating income support, and are deducted from the benefit payment. So, for example, if your maintenance payment goes up, your income support will go down correspondingly. If you live in rented accommodation, you can get housing benefit to cover all eligible rent. For owner-occupiers, income support covers half the eligible mortgage interest payments for the first 16 weeks, and then the whole of the eligible mortgage interest payments. If you receive income support you are also entitled to free school meals, free milk and vitamins for pregnant women and children under five, help with NHS costs (free

prescriptions, dental check-ups and sight tests), and maximum council tax benefit.

- **Family credit.** This is a means-tested benefit available to families with dependent children if you work for 16 or more hours a week. It doesn't help with housing costs or council tax, but you may be eligible for housing benefit for rent payments and council tax benefit. The adult payment is the same for a lone parent and a couple, and payments are made for children according to age. If your earnings rise, the benefit payment goes down by 70 per cent of the rise in earnings. One parent benefit and child benefit are ignored in calculating family credit entitlement. A childcare disregard introduced in October 1994 is available to all parents eligible for family credit who have a child under 11 years of age and who use a registered child minder or day nursery. You will be compensated for 70 per cent of childcare costs (up to costs of a maximum of £40) through your family credit payments. Examples of how the payment works are shown below:

  If you earn £60 per week and pay £45 per week in childcare expenses, your earnings for family credit purposes become £60 minus £40 (the maximum) = £20 per week. The decrease in your income of £40 will be compensated by an increase in family credit of 70% of £40 = £28 per week.

  If you earn £60 per week and pay £20 per week in childcare expenses, your earnings for family credit purposes become £60 minus £20 = £40 per week – a decrease of £20. This is compensated by an increase in family credit of 70% of £20 = £14 per week.

Receiving family credit does not make you eligible for free school meals, but reduced-price milk is available if you have a baby under one. You will get help with NHS costs. You are allowed to keep the first £15 of any maintenance payments before it reduces your family credit entitlement. If you are awarded family credit you will receive payments over a six-month period, during which time the amount cannot be altered even if your circumstances change. If your earnings are too high for you to receive family credit you may still receive some benefits such as Housing Benefit and Council tax Benefit.

Take-up rates for family credit are low – according to a DSS survey in 1992, only around 50 to 60 per cent of eligible lone parents claim, possibly because it is complicated and difficult to apply for.

- **Housing benefit and council tax benefit.** These means-tested benefits can provide help with rent and council tax.
- **Tax.** If you have a dependent child and are unmarried, separated or divorced you can claim the additional personal allowance which will bring you to the level of the married couple's allowance. Unlike many other countries, there is no tax relief for childcare for under fives (for lone parents or couples).
- **Child maintenance.** If you've been married and are now separated or divorced, you may be eligible for child maintenance payments or alternatively responsible for making payments to your ex-partner. In 1991, maintenance payments from former partners accounted for only seven per cent of all income for lone parents. At that time, the whole maintenance payment was counted as income in calculating means-tested benefits, so there was little incentive to seek maintenance from absent partners because it didn't leave you any better off, and it was often an unreliable source of income. Since April 1992, you've been allowed to keep the first £15 per week of maintenance payments before any deduction from family credit, housing benefit or council tax benefit is made. The Child Support Agency (CSA), set up in

August 1993, determines how much an absent parent should pay, based on the cost of looking after children, any other children either parent may have, and the income of both parents, allowing for tax, national insurance and essential expenses such as rent or mortgage costs. While the CSA tries to make sure that absent parents paying child support maintenance have sufficient income to live on, the reality is that it's very difficult to manage the financial commitments involved in contributing to two households rather than one. Parents in this position may find they need to increase their income, for example by working overtime or getting a better paid job.

ISSUES FOR DIFFERENT LONE PARENTS

Lone parents form a very diverse group. How you have come to be on your own with children will affect your particular circumstances and probably your attitude to working.

SINGLE, NEVER MARRIED

If you've never had a partner but have brought up your child single-handed from the start, you will have had to make decisions about whether or not to work, and how best to combine it with parenting. As a group, young single mothers have little training or work experience, and the poorly paid jobs open to many of them may mean it's not worth their while to work. For women who are older and established in a career who then choose to have a child on their own, the situation is very different. They will be able to command a high enough salary to allow them a lifestyle which makes it relatively easier to combine work and parenting, including support at home and a wide range of childcare options.

SEPARATION, DIVORCE AND BEREAVEMENT

Becoming a lone parent because of separation or divorce, or through bereavement, is likely to be a traumatic experience. At a time when you're grappling with your own and your children's emotional trauma, as well as a number of practical problems around legal matters, money, housing or your ex-partner, work problems may be difficult to face. Find out about any benefits, maintenance payments, widows pensions or work pensions you may be entitled to.

- **If you're already employed** – you will at least have the stability of a work routine and some income, although it may well fall far short of the combined income which you've been living on up to now. A job with which you've coped well so far may be much harder to manage when you also have to do absolutely everything at home and for the children. This may be particularly true for fathers who find themselves suddenly having to take the strain at home as well as at work.

- **If you've been at home** – it can be a daunting prospect to find you suddenly need a job to support your family when previously you've been looking after young children while being financially supported by your partner. You may feel very ill-equipped and lacking the confidence to get yourself together to compete for hard-to-find jobs at a time when there's so much else going on in your life. Yet some people find work is a useful distraction, providing the stability and structure they need when they're going through a difficult period.

"When John died suddenly, the bottom dropped out of my world. I hadn't worked since before my elder son was born – more than eight years – and was very anxious at the thought of working again. I'd lost all my confidence and felt I'd never be able to cope. But getting a

job took me out of myself and stopped me sitting around moping at home. "

Sally (31) sales assistant

It may sound all too easy to say, but try not to panic. Take things one step at a time, and don't feel rushed into decisions about work which you may later regret. If you've already got a job, but need some time to sort things out at home and be there for the children, ask for some compassionate leave, or if that's not possible, unpaid leave rather than quitting your job on impulse. You could talk through your situation at work and see if they will agree to changing your work pattern to fit in better with your additional family commitments (see 'Family-friendly employers', page 7). If you haven't been working but now feel panicked into taking the first job that comes along, take time to think through your options, including the possibility of training or returner's courses.

LONE FATHERS

Only one in ten of all lone parents is a father, and there are particular attitudes towards them. Most people believe that while lone mothers should stay home to look after their children, fathers in the same position should go out to work rather than become househusbands. Fathers who do decide to stay at home to care for young children may well be confronted with negative attitudes from those people who see it as 'unmanly', believe men are no good at day-to-day care of children, or feel a man's responsibility is to bring in a wage.

Men may find themselves on their own with children through different circumstances, and whether they have chosen to become lone fathers will have a large impact on how they experience it. If a man has actively sought or agreed to have his children living with him after separation or divorce, he may feel better prepared and in more control than one whose partner has died, or has left him and the children. Those with a secure, well-paid job and supportive family network will obviously be better able to cope. Lone fathers are more likely to be offered help from friends, family and neighbours because they're seen as more helpless, although offers may dwindle with time. It may be more difficult for fathers caring for their young children to link into the usual local networks such as 'mother and toddler groups', 'one o'clock clubs' and NCT support groups, where the majority of parents attending are mothers, and find the peer support of other fathers. Things are changing, though, with unemployment affecting men more than women, and fathers in general taking more responsibility for the care of their children, so that it's more usual to see fathers dropping their children at playschool or school and picking them up at the end of the day.

Studies show that family income decreases when fathers become lone parents and this is not only accounted for by the loss of the partner's earnings, but also because the father actually brings home less money, and expenditure on items such as childcare rises. Overtime may be limited by family responsibilities, and career opportunities curtailed by lack of flexibility or ability to put in long hours.

"My career definitely suffered when I stopped work for a while to look after my three year old. My wife left us out of the blue, and at the time my way of coping was to give up my well-paid job and take on full-time responsibility for Simon and the home. I didn't get myself together enough to work again till more than a year later, by which time I'd missed out on promotion and lost some momentum in my career. I don't think I ever quite made up the lost ground, but on the other hand I gained an enormous amount from having that time with my son."

Bill (30) account manager

Lone fathers are more likely to be bringing up older children, quite often teenagers, in which case they have fewer childcare needs. They're much more likely than mothers on their own to be in a paid job, and that work is likely to be better paid. More than a third of lone fathers find they have to give up work at some point to care for their children full-time, but most return to work, and overall five out of six lone fathers have a job. Employers may take a less flexible line with male employees than they do with female workers, expecting them to put in unreasonably long hours and put work before family commitments. The growing numbers of employers offering 'family friendly' workplaces are realising that in order to compete successfully for the best qualified staff, and retain them, they need to be more flexible about the way in which people work (see 'Family friendly employment', page 7) and this applies to both male and female workers.

CHILDCARE FOR LONE PARENTS

Like other working parents, you will need to find good quality and affordable childcare for your children while you're at work. The different types of childcare that may be available to you are described in Chapter 7, together with some suggestions about how to find the care which best suits you and the needs of your family.

Some particular issues which may affect you as a lone parent are discussed below.

IF YOUR INCOME IS VERY LOW

Lone parents as a group tend to have money problems, and having to meet childcare costs from one income rather than two may limit your options even though your needs are very pressing.

Many lone parents say they would choose to work if they had access to good quality and affordable childcare, but the reality for many of them is that the cost of childcare eats into too great a proportion of their earnings. The childcare disregard introduced in October 1994 goes some way to helping with this (see page 186 for more details) but will still leave many families with childcare needs that are difficult to afford.

You may be offered a subsidised place at a local authority or voluntary sector day nursery or with a childminder, although in some parts of the country the majority of such places are taken by priority families with special needs. Your employer may provide help with childcare, in the form of childcare vouchers, an on-site nursery, or a subsidised place at a local nursery, and these benefits are sometimes particularly targeted at lone parents or other employees with high need.

Another way round the problem may be for your family to look after your child, either full-time or to supplement other childcare. Many parents feel they want to pay something for this, but it may be more affordable than the alternatives.

"Jason goes to playschool every morning; I work flexi-time so can take him on my way to work. My mum picks him up from there, gives him lunch and looks after him till I get back around six. She loves having him but I insist on paying her something. The problem is school holidays when playschool is closed. I think it's too much for mum to have him all day, so he goes to different friends for odd days and we just muddle through."

Terrence (26) clerk

YOUR EX-PARTNER

Even though you're no longer living together, it may be possible to share some childcare with your ex-partner. If they live near enough and depending on their own work commitments, they may be able to pick children up from the childminder or school some days, have them some weekends or holidays, and take more on during a crisis. It's a good way of ensuring children keep in touch with both of you, and you may feel more confident about the care they will be getting.

"Dave might have been dreadful as a husband, but he was always a good father. Daniel really benefited by spending time with us both after we divorced, and I was much happier for him to go to Dave than to the childminder."

Jane (36) teacher

"When we split up, we agreed that the children would live with Jenny but I'd have them every other weekend, and for two weeks in the school holidays. I was determined not to lose touch with the kids, and in fact it's worked out extremely well. They benefit from seeing both of us, and I know Jenny appreciates the time off she gets."

Richard (37) accountant

Communication between you is the key to making this work. It may help if you:

- Agree between you who will have the children when, and keep to the arrangements as far as possible;
- Give each other plenty of notice if the usual arrangement has to change;
- Co-ordinate when you will take annual holidays, if you need to be away on business, or other events which you have some control over.

GETTING SUPPORT FOR YOURSELF

There's no two ways about it, being a lone parent can be exhausting and you will need all the support you can get if you're going to hold down a job too. Go for childcare which gives you the least hassle and the maximum support, as far as your budget allows. Help in your own home may offer the most benefits – you won't have to get the children up and out in the morning, and may get some help with household chores like washing and ironing or at least tidying up. Live-in help may give you the greatest flexibility in terms of not having to watch the clock quite so much, and offers some babysitting, too. You won't have the problem of not being able to take a young sitter home after your evening out because of having no one to stay with your children, and you can be as late as you like because they can just go to bed. Of course, live-in help can be very expensive, but for older children an au-pair may work well and works out quite cheap (see page 131).

You will have childcare needs over and above those which allow you to do a paid job if you are going to remain sane. It's good to be able to do the weekly shop or go to the doctor without always having a child in tow, and you also need time off to relax, do your own thing or enjoy yourself with friends.

"The worst thing is that feeling of being trapped. Once Lucy's in bed in the evening, I'm stuck. It's not that I want a hectic social life – it would sometimes be good just to go round Sainsbury's or swim at the local pool without the hassle and expense of organising a sitter. It's the sort of thing I took for granted before Mike died."

Josie (28) market researcher

Babysitting may become expensive, because it's not so easy for you to reciprocate if there's no one at home to look after your own children! One way round this is to have your children's friends to stay overnight in return for any sitting they do for you. Your family may also be happy to babysit if they live close by.

SURVIVAL CHECKLIST FOR WORKING LONE PARENTS

- Accept all offers of help, and buy as much in as you can afford.
- Build up a strong support network of people you can rely on.
- If you're going through the process of separation or divorce, or have been bereaved, take things slowly, one step at a time.
- Get advice about benefits, pensions or maintenance entitlements and make sure you claim.
- Look for training or retraining opportunities to maximise your earning capacity.
- Cut down on guilt feelings and focus on the positive aspects of your situation.
- Go for childcare that offers the maximum stress relief within your budget.
- Look for a family-friendly employer or convert your existing workplace into one.

11 MAKING TIME FOR EVERYONE

RECOGNISING OVERLOAD

Working parents often feel there are simply not enough hours in the day to fit everything in. Balancing the demands of work and home is never easy but there is a difference between being busy and being over-burdened to the point where life feels like a treadmill, leaving you no time at all to enjoy your job or being with your family.

So how can you avoid this kind of overload? The first thing to understand is that stress in itself is not bad – a certain amount of stress can help us work more efficiently, more innovatively. But too much stress can work against us instead of for us, it can make us less efficient, more indecisive – and certainly more irritable.

When we are under a lot of stress we often make things worse for ourselves by the things we do and the way we feel. We may get into a spiral trying to cope with everything, while feeling that we are failing to do anything properly. So we might feel guilty about not being a good parent. We might feel guilty about not giving our best at work. Yet these kind of feelings can just add to our stress.

Recognising when we are under too much stress is essential. We all need to watch out for the warning signs: constant tiredness, difficulty sleeping, more headaches than usual, digestive disturbances, loss of appetite or a craving for comfort foods, panic or anxiety attacks, lack of interest in sex, short-temperedness.

By themselves, each of these symptoms does not necessarily mean you are over-stressed. But if you experience several of them, and they persist for a while, the chances are that you need to look at what is going on in your life.

It is well known that some events are difficult for most of us to handle. Change of any kind – whether it is change we have been looking forward to or dreading – is one kind of pressure that makes demands on all of us. Change is part of life, and most of the time we adjust to it. But it is when you are trying to cope with more than a couple of changes at once (e.g. finding someone new to look after your child, handling different responsibilities at work, visiting a relative in hospital and missing your best friend because she has moved hundreds of miles away) that you begin to feel overburdened.

ARE YOU UNDER STRESS?

Ask yourself the following questions. The more 'yes's' you have in the first three sections and the more 'no's' in the last, the more stress you are likely to be under.

Work

- Have you changed jobs, employer or location?
- Have you taken on new responsibilities or been promoted?
- Have you been demoted or moved sideways?
- Do you have a long journey to work?
- Do your hours clash with your family responsibilities?
- Is your work boring?
- Do you feel you lack control over what you do at work?
- Are you irritated by your colleagues?

Family

- Have you moved house recently?

- Has anyone close to you died or been seriously ill?
- Have you recently separated or divorced?
- Have you recently had a baby?
- Has a relative come to live with you?
- Is anyone close to you in trouble/at loggerheads with you?

If you have a partner

- Do you argue a lot?
- Do you find it difficult to talk to each other?
- Do you have financial worries?
- Do you disagree about bringing up the children?

You

- Do those close to you understand when you are upset and needy?
- Do you feel loved by family and friends?
- Do you have close friends outside the family?
- Is there someone you can talk to about problems at work or home?
- Do you allow time for exercise or relaxation?
- Do you eat properly?
- Have you still got your sense of humour?
- Do you give yourself little rewards from time to time?

DEALING WITH STRESS

One of the things which makes people feel even more stressed is a sense that things are out of their control. Being in a constant rush, feeling that you have too much on your plate, will make matters worse. So if you want to de-stress your life and make time for the things you *really* want to do, you need to take a look at the way you use your time now, and the way you would prefer to use it.

MANAGING YOUR TIME

Do you know where your time goes? Draw up a list of what you do in a typical day. Include everything, no matter how trivial, and then go back through it.

Look at each item in turn and ask yourself three key questions:

- Do I really need to do this?
- Could I do this more efficiently?
- Could someone else be doing this?

Clearly every parent will have a different list of 'must do's' and 'can do withouts'. You might hate the idea of leaving the breakfast things out all day, or the beds unmade. Or you might feel that gaining time in the morning is worth having to face those chores at night.

Once you know where your time goes from day to day you can also begin to think about the balance of time over a longer period. In a week, for instance, how much time do you spend on household tasks, how much time with your children, how much time at work? Do you have time for yourself and your own interests? If you are part of a couple, how much time do you have for the relationship?

Now think about the way you would rather allocate your time. You might rather spend less time at work and more with the children. In order to achieve that you would have to think of ways you could cut down your work hours. Even if that isn't possible right now, you will at least know what your goal for the future could be, and you might find other ways of making more time for being with the children. If you are spending a lot of time on household chores , for example, you might want to rethink your priorities on the home front.

Or you might want to rethink the time your spend sleeping.

Some parents find that getting up half an hour earlier in the morning means they can sit down to breakfast with their children. Breakfast then becomes more than a feeding time. Others, however, feel that the extra time in bed makes all the difference between a calm and a grumpy start to the day.

KNOWING WHEN TO SAY NO

If you feel you have too much to do, either at home or at work, it is worth asking yourself whether you have brought any of the pressure on yourself. Sometimes it is the things we agree to do in a weak moment, which prove to be the last straw. We end up resenting the time we are spending on a task we never really wanted to do – whether that's baking a cake for the nursery bring and buy sale or writing a report that wasn't really our job in the first place.

If you find it hard to say 'no', start by giving yourself time to think the request through. When you are asked if you'll do something, say 'I'm not sure. I'll think about it and let you know.' If the person persists in getting an answer then and there, say 'In that case, I'm afraid it will have to be no.'

Once you have thought the situation through you can decide whether to say no, or whether to offer a compromise. For example you could say 'I won't have time to bake a cake, but I could buy one and donate it to the sale instead.'

If you decide to say 'no', you need to be firm and clear in your refusal. If the person making the request tries to get you to change your mind, simply repeat yourself, without being drawn into a long discussion. If you make excuses – 'I'm no good at making cakes' – the other person will just try to persuade you that it doesn't matter. So keep it simple, don't apologise for saying no, and don't waver. Just say, 'I'm too busy at the moment.'

Once you have established your priorities, you need to be able to delegate some of the things which don't have to be done by you. As your children get older there is no reason why they can't begin to do some of the chores – even small children can be taught to put things away when they have finished with them. Older ones can wash up, make beds, dust and vacuum, load the washing machine.

Taking the time to teach them some basic households skills will save you time in the long run. More than this, though, you will be getting them ready for the future, when they will leave home and have to look after themselves.

SPENDING TIME WITH YOUR CHILDREN

Sometimes working parents get so caught up in the day-to-day routines necessary to keep everything ticking over that there never seems to be any time when they can simply enjoy being with their children.

One approach is to try to limit the number of outside activities in your children's lives. There are now groups and clubs offering so many things – gymnastics, football, rugby, ice-skating, french, tap, ballet, chess, Cubs, Brownies, drama, music and so on – that it can be all too easy to find that you spend most of your time ferrying your children from one activity to another. Children need time just to be children, and you need time to be with them just to enjoy their company.

Because time is so precious for most working parents, some people like the idea of quality time. This is based on the premise that the amount of time you spend with your children is less important than the quality of that time. In many ways that is bound to be true – after all, you could spend all day with a child but if you were too busy or preoccupied to pay them any attention, you might as well not be there at all.

The trouble with the idea of quality time is that children don't always want to play along. If you come home from work, firmly intending to spend an hour or so doing something with your child before supper, it can be upsetting to find they are more interested in watching television or playing with their building bricks than having you talk about their day at school or read them a story.

It can be even more upsetting if, later on, they become demanding and/or fractious at the point when you had just decided to put your feet up and take a breather.

If your child is being cared for in your own home, you need to take your lead from them. Let them set the pace. If they want to watch television, watch with them. If they are playing with bricks, sit on the floor and wait to be invited to join in. Don't expect to come in from the outside and monopolise the situation.

If you are bringing your child home from a nursery, school or childminder, give them time to settle down before suggesting activities you might share. They may need to make the transition from one place to another, just as you make the transition from home to work and back again. Sometimes having a set routine can help the process, offering a drink or snack, for instance.

Older children can be particularly infuriating when it comes to letting you into their lives. One moment they will be monosyllabic about their day, the next they will be demanding help with homework immediately.

Rather than having fixed ideas about how you will spend time with your children, it may be better to settle for a more flexible approach. This means learning to know when a child would welcome your interest, when a child needs your full attention, and when you can get on with something else, such as preparing an evening meal or having a quiet five minutes to yourself.

At the same time, remember that you don't have to drop everything the minute a child demands your time. If you are in the middle of something else, depending on the urgency and the age of the child, you can suggest they wait, try to sort it out themselves, or get someone else to help.

Sometimes you can suggest an alternative. You might not be able to help finish a jigsaw if you happen to be peeling potatoes at the time. But you could tell a story, or join in the songs your child has just learned at nursery.

Of course, when you have more than one child, the situation is more complicated. Each child may end up competing with the others for your attention. One way round this may be to have a routine which gives you time with each child in turn. How you sort this out depends on the age and amenability of the children, and whether or not there is anyone else around to lend a hand. Staggering bath times and bed times can help. Another idea, if your partner or someone else is around to help, is to take just one child with you when you do the supermarket shop, for example, or take the washing to the launderette.

THINGS TO REMIND YOURSELF OF

- Your family will love you even if you refuse their demands now and then.
- You have rights, needs and desires too.
- You don't have to be superhuman – it won't really matter if you feed your family instant meals from time to time instead of home-baked ones, all they will notice is whether they are served with love.

- Your child won't suffer if you don't iron his T-shirts, are grumpy occasionally or forget to wave goodbye one morning.
- Children will benefit if they grow up learning how to take care of themselves.

TIME WITH YOUR PARTNER

Finding time to be with your children – or at least finding the time to be with them when they want to be with you – may seem hard enough. Finding time to be with your partner, if you have one, may seem even more difficult. Yet it is important because the way the two of you relate together is bound to affect the whole family.

Some couples find it helps to plan ahead, writing down a date in the diary and then making any necessary arrangements. It sounds desperately formal, but it may be the only way to make sure that you make space for time together, and by planning ahead you can sort out who will look after the children so you can be alone.

Would a member of your family have the children for a while, or come to your home to look after them? Are the children old enough to go to play at a friend's house for the afternoon, or to sleep over for the night? Do you know someone who can be trusted to babysit, either for money or in return for you offering to babysit another time?

You don't have to go out for an evening: you could catch an afternoon film at the local cinema or go for a walk. You could plan a lazy morning, going back to bed with the papers and a pot of tea.

Once your children are past the baby stage you need to let them know that your bedroom is your own special place. Of course that doesn't mean your children are never allowed into your bed. You can make it clear that they are welcome at certain times but even then, as they get older, you can ask them to knock before dashing in. You may also want to put a lock on the door to make sure a child doesn't barge in during your most intimate moments.

Children need to know that adults need time and space together and it makes sense to be open about this. As children get older, their bedtime tends to get later. This, in turn, may encroach on the time you and your partner have together. Some parents suggest their children go off to their bedroom to listen to music, read a book or play games, explaining that adults need time alone together once in a while.

FINDING TIME FOR YOURSELF

When you are working out how you want to allocate your time it is important to remember to include time just for yourself. You may want to schedule time when you can go for a swim (without taking a toddler, two arms bands, spare nappies and the rest of the paraphernalia) or half an hour to soak in the bath without anyone banging on the door to ask what you've done with their football strip, or just the chance to watch your favourite television programme in peace.

As a working parent you will spend a lot of time meeting other people's needs: you need to create some space for yourself when, for a little while at least, no one is making demands on you.

If you have younger children you will need help to make this space. If you have a partner you could arrange to take it in turns to give the other 'time out' from parenting. When it is your turn to 'switch off', arrange to do something that makes you feel good – visit friends, have a lie-in, or do absolutely nothing at all.

If you don't have a partner, 'me-time' might be harder to arrange. You might have a friend with a child of the same age. Could you take it in turns to give each other some free time? Is there anyone in your family who might help? If you pay for childcare, could you afford to pay your carer a little more to work later or at the weekend, to give you some time to yourself?

WHO IS THERE FOR YOU?

Even if you have a partner, it is worth reminding yourself that no one person can supply all your needs – and it isn't fair to expect them to do so. It may be a good idea to review your own support network, and see if you can make it work better for you.

Draw a circle and put your name in the middle. Now draw smaller circles around the outside. Inside write headings for different aspects of your life including the parts you sometimes need help with. Your headings might include work, friendships, sex, family, relationships, chores, childcare, transport, social life, interests.

Then, next to each of these circles, list the names of people who are involved in that part of your life. When you have put down everyone you can think of, see how balanced it looks. Perhaps the same name crops up over and over again. Maybe there aren't many names at all. So how could you widen your support network.

Perhaps you could make contact with friends you've been out of touch with for a while? Perhaps you could think about joining a support group, like Parents At Work, for example. Perhaps all the things you've felt too busy to do – start an evening class, go to Neighbourhood Watch meetings, phone your friends – are things you need to find time to do. The more people you can talk to about your problems or ask for help in a crisis, the less pressure you will feel under.

BEING NICE TO YOURSELF

People often find it hard to give themselves a pat on the back for a job well done. All too often, they focus on the times when they didn't do as well as they had hoped, not on the good moments when everything went as planned. It helps to remind yourself from time to time of all the things you can do well; perhaps you are an ace story-teller or you have a great telephone manner.

It can also be a good idea to make a list of all the things you like doing, and make sure you give yourself time to do them now and then. Your list might include going to see a new film or getting a video, walking in the countryside or supporting your favourite football team.

LOOK AFTER YOURSELF

When you are busy there is always the temptation to skip meals or eat on the run. But it is better to have a proper breakfast – even if it is only a glass of juice and a slice or two of wholemeal toast – than to find yourself snacking on biscuits when your energy levels plummet mid-morning. Even if you find yourself relying more on convenience foods than you would if you had more time, make sure you get plenty of fresh fruit and vegetables and try to keep a healthy balance (see page 40).

Exercise is a good way of releasing tension and relieving stress. Find something you like doing so that you are less likely to give up after a couple of sessions.

Alternative or complementary therapies can also help you relax or handle stress better. Some you can try for yourself, such as meditation, creative visualisation, and massage. Others therapies, which you may have to pay for, include yoga, aromatherapy and reflexology. Your local library will have a selection of books on these subjects or you could ask about local classes. The Health Education Authority publishes a useful book on complementary therapies, the *HEA Guide to Complementary Medicine and Therapies* by Anne Woodham.

RELAXATION

Relaxation can be learned, just like any other technique. The exercise below is one of the most simple ways of relaxing and will take about 15 minutes. It can also be used to help you get to sleep at night.

- Find a place where you can be alone, warm and quiet.
- Lie on a bed or the floor, or sit in a chair with a high back to support your head and neck. Settle yourself comfortably and close your eyes.
- Begin by breathing out first. Then breathe in easily, just as much as you need. Now breathe out slowly, with a slight sigh. Do this once more, slowly ... in ... and out ... and as you breathe out, feel the tension begin to drain away. Then go back to your normal breathing: even, quiet, steady.
- Next direct your thoughts to each part of your body in turn, to the muscles and the joints.
  - Now think about your left foot. Your toes are still. Become aware of how heavy your foot feels on the floor.
  - Now think about your right foot. Now both your feet, your toes, your ankles are starting to relax.
  - Now think about your legs. Let your thighs and knees roll downwards. Let your legs feel heavy and relaxed.
  - Now think about your back and spine. Let the tension

drain away. Each time you breathe out, relax your back and spine a little more.

- Let your stomach muscles become soft and loose. Feel your stomach rise and fall as you breathe gently. Each time you breathe out, let your chest relax a little more.

- Think about the fingers of your left hand. Let them lie limp and quite still. Now the fingers of the right hand. They are relaxed and still.

- Let the feeling of relaxation spread up your arms. They are getting heavier. Let your shoulders go, let them drop, even further than you thought they could.

- Now think about your neck. Feel the tension melt away from your neck and shoulders.

- Now just check to see that all these part of your body are still relaxed – your feet, your legs, back and spine, sto-mach, hands, arms, neck, shoulders. Keep your breathing soft and gentle. Every time you breathe out, feel a little more tension drain away.

- Now think about your face. Let your forehead feel wide and relaxed. Let your eyebrows drop slightly. Let go of the tension round your eyes. Your eyes are still and relaxed. Let your jaw relax, teeth slightly apart. Feel the relief of letting go.

- Let your tongue drop down to the bottom of your mouth. Feel your throat relax. Your lips are just lightly touching. Let all the muscles in your face unwind. Let all the tension go.

• Now think of your body as a whole again. Feel the all-over sensation of letting go, of being still and relaxed. Listen to your breathing ... in ... and out.... Let your body become looser and heavier each time you breathe out.

• Now continue for a little longer. Enjoy this quiet time for relaxation.

- When you want to come back, start by slowly wriggling your hands and feet. When you are ready, open your eyes, and stay quiet and still for a little while. Stretch, if you want to, or yawn, and slowly start to move again.

GETTING AWAY FROM IT ALL

Having a holiday away from home and work may seem an ideal way of reducing your stress levels and getting on an even keel again.

WITHOUT THE CHILDREN

Certainly some working parents say that having an occasional weekend break *without the children* works wonders. Of course, if money is tight this kind of solution may seem beyond your reach. But before you dismiss the idea altogether, make sure you have thought of all the possibilities.

Is there someone your child knows and you trust who would have your child to stay for a weekend? Even if you couldn't afford to go away, just spending a couple of days alone at home might seem like a holiday.

Or could you swap with someone: they could stay at your home and look after your children, while you stayed in theirs for a couple of nights.

Older children enjoy having sleepovers: if you can cope with the giggling and the midnight feasts one weekend, would another family reciprocate next time?

Some families are lucky enough to have mother's helps or nannies who become such good friends that they are happy to take their charges to meet their own families. Others might be prepared to work over a weekend for time off in lieu and/or an extra payment.

During the summer a number of organisations offer residential activity holidays for children. They are not cheap, and not all children enjoy the thought of going away to share a dormitory with people they don't know. But many children love the experience and some parents feel it is well worth the expense.

FAMILY HOLIDAYS

If you work, family holidays may be one of the few times when you can all spend time together, enjoying each other's company – providing you have planned a holiday that will give you the break you need and the children something they will enjoy.

Your choice of holiday will depend on what you can afford, the age of your children and the kind of things you all like to do. You might like sight-seeing: young children would probably be happier on a beach. Teenagers tend to sulk if there are no shops/discos/other teenagers within striking distance.

If this is the first holiday you are taking with a toddler, for example, you will have to consider the pros and cons from a different viewpoint. It will be no fun to spend two weeks in constant dread that your children are going to fall off a balcony, hurtle down a steep flight of stairs or drown in a swimming pool the minute you take your eyes off them.

If you are planning to go abroad, you will also have to consider the climate. You may be a sun-lover, but young children in particular often react badly in heat. Even if you are lucky enough to have a child who doesn't get heat rash – or tetchy because it is too hot to sleep at night – you will be the one slapping on Factor 25, and trying to make him stay in the shade and keep his sunhat on.

On the other hand, two wet weeks somewhere in Britain may be even more stressful. If you are planning to stay closer to home, you need to think about the kind of things you will be able to do if it is cold or rains as being holed up with young children, without the usual distractions and amusements of home, is no fun.

Many families choose to go self-catering, either abroad or at home. This has the advantage of flexibility in deciding what and when you will eat. It may give you more space than sharing a hotel bedroom. The downside is that it may feel less like a holiday than going somewhere where someone else is paid to cook, wash-up, make the beds and so on.

Another question you need to think about is whether you will go alone or with other people. Some parents join up with grand-parents, some with friends who have children of the same age. Some families can afford to pay a nanny, au-pair or mother's help to come on holiday with them.

If you are considering one of these possibilities it is worth sorting out a few things before you book up. How much help in terms of childcare or babysitting will the arrangement give you, and will this outweigh the additional stress of having to get on with other people?

Once again, the answer will depend on your particular circum-stances. Having your in-laws to babysit may give you a rare chance to go out in the evenings. Sharing with another family may mean that the children keep each other amused all day while you relax with a book. On the other hand you may find other people a bit much every morning over breakfast, and your children may fall out with their friends on day two, leaving you with an awkward situation to handle.

If you do decide to go with other people talk things through with the them so that no one feels they are being taken advantage of. If you are taking an au pair, nanny or mother's help you need to explain how you want to split the childcare and how much time she can expect for herself, both during the day and in the evenings. You need to discuss with other relatives how much help they expect to give during the day, if any, and whether they are willing to babysit in the evenings. If you are going with a family you need to find out whether they expect you to do things together most of the time, or if they would prefer just to meet up in the evenings or take it in turns to have the children during the day.

The whole point about having a holiday is that it should give you a chance to relax and unwind, rather than adding to the stresses of every day life. There is an increasing number of holiday packages both at home and abroad which offer parents a variety of services to help them enjoy their break. These range from baby-listening in hotels, so that you can, in theory, have an evening meal in the restaurant while your children sleep, to clubs for children where they can, under supervision, play games or listen to stories and be kept amused and busy for part of the day. If these services are available they will be mentioned in the brochures or promotional literature.

ADDRESSES OF USEFUL ORGANISATIONS

CHILDCARE

CACHE (Council for Awards in Children's Care and Education)
8 Chequer Street, St Albans, Hertfordshire, AL1 3X7. Tel 01727 847 636

Daycare Trust
Wesley House, 4 Wild Court, London WC2B 5AU. Tel 0171 405 5617. *Provides information on quality daycare and promotes local childcare information services.*

Employers for Childcare
Cowley House, Little College Street, London SW1P 3XS. Tel 0171 233 0355. *Members include leading UK employers who have come together to urge the government to take a lead in establishing a national policy and strategy on childcare.*

Kids' Club Network
279-81 Whitechapel Road, London E1 1BY. Tel 0171 247 3009. *Promotes the provision of out-of-school and holiday care for children up to 12 years, and provides information on setting up local schemes.*

Nannytax
PO Box 988, Brighton, BN2 1BY. Tel 01273 626256. *A nationwide payroll service for parents employing a nanny. For an annual fee they will keep tax records, provide payslips which show the deductions made, and provide advice about when tax and NI payments are due and for how much.*

National Childcare Campaign/ Daycare Trust
(See Daycare Trust). *Information on childcare, including how to set up a community nursery and organise local childcare campaigns.*

National Childminding Association
8 Masons Hill, Bromley, Kent BR2 9EX. Tel 0181 466 0200. *Information for both childminders and parents; promotes the interests of childminders and seeks to improve the quality of childcare provided by them through resources and training.*

Nursery World
Childcare Classified Dept., The Schoolhouse Workshop, 51 Calthorpe Street, London WC1X 0HH. Tel 0171 837 7244. *Takes classified advertisements for nannies.*

Parents at Work
77 Holloway Road, London N7 8JZ. Tel 0171 700 5771/2. *Provides information for parents on choosing and finding the best care for their children; promotes local support groups for sharing advice about coping with employment and childrearing; provides information to policy- and decision-makers about the needs of working parents and their children.*

Pre-school Playgroup Association (PPA)
61-63 King's Cross Road, London WC1X 9LL. Tel 0171 837 0991

The Lady
39-40 Bedford Street, London WC2E 9ER. Tel 0171 379 4717. *Takes classified advertisements for nannies.*

Working for Childcare
77 Holloway Road, London N7 8JZ. Tel 0171 700 0281. *Campaigns for all forms of good quality childcare, and advises on workplace schemes.*

EDUCATION AND SUPPORT FOR PARENTING

CRY-SIS
BM Cry-sis, London WC1N 3XX. Tel 0171 404 5011. *Self-help and support for families with excessively crying, sleepless and demanding children.*

La Leche League of Great Britain
BM 3424, London WC1N 3XX. Tel 0171 242 1278. *Help and information for women who want to breastfeed. Offers personal counselling and local groups.*

Meet-A-Mum Association
14 Willis Road, Croydon, Surrey CR0 2XX. Tel 0181 665 0357. *Support and help for women suffering from postnatal depression, feeling isolated and tired after having a baby, or just in need of a friend to share problems. Local groups and one-to-one contact.*

National Childbirth Trust
Alexandra House, Oldham Terrace, London W3 6NH. Tel 0181 992 8637. *Promotes education for parenthood; offers postnatal counselling and support.*

Parents Anonymous
Tel 0171 263 8918/ 0181 689 3136. *A telephone helpline for all parents under stress.*

EDUCATION AND TRAINING

National Extension College
18 Brooklands Avenue, Cambridge CB2 2HN. Tel 01223 316644. *Offers correspondence courses on a wide range of subjects up to degree level.*

National Women's Register
9 Bank Plain, Norwich NR2 4SL. Tel 01603 765392. *Provides the chance to meet with other women locally for support and stimulation.*

Open University
Walton Hall, Milton Keynes MK7 6AA. Tel 01908 274066.
Correspondence courses open to anyone, with TV and radio lectures, tutorials and residential summer schools (no childcare facilities).

EMPLOYMENT AND MATERNITY RIGHTS

Childcare Vouchers Scheme
Luncheon Vouchers Limited, 50 Vauxhall Bridge Road, London SW1V 2RS. Tel 0171 834 6666

Equal Opportunities Commission
Overseas House, Quay Street, Manchester M3 3HN. Tel 0161 833 9244. *General equal opportunities work; may be able to help if you want to challenge a demand to pay back maternity pay.*

Home-Run
Active Information, 79 Black Lion Lane, London W6 9BG. Tel 0181 741 2440. *Newsletter for people who work from home.*

Maternity Alliance
15 Britannia Street, London WC1X 9JP. Tel 0171 837 1265. *Information on all aspects of maternity care and rights. Advice on benefits, maternity rights at work.*

New Ways to Work
309 Upper Street, London N1 2TY. Tel 0171 226 4026. *Information on flexible working and job-sharing.*

OwnBase
68 First Avenue, Bush Hill Park, Enfield, Middlesex EN1 1BN. *A network and newsletter for people who work from home.*

Women Returners' Network
8 John Adam Street, London WC2N 6EZ. Tel 0171 839 8188. *Provides information about courses to update you; self-assessment and career planning.*

HEALTH

ASH
109 Gloucester Place, London W1H 3PH. Tel 0171 935 3519. *Assists smokers wishing to stop and promotes non-smoking as a norm. Offers information and resources for the public.*

British Homeopathic Association
27a Devonshire Street, London W1N 1RJ. Tel 0171 935 2163

Health and Safety Executive
Baynards House, Chepstow Place,
London W2 4TF. Tel 0171 243 6000

Health Education Authority
Hamilton house, Mabledon Place,
London WC1H 9TX. Tel 0171 383
3833. *A special health authority with
responsibility for providing advice and
support about health education to the
general public. Publishes a wide range of
resources.*

Quit
102 Gloucester Place, London W1H
3DA.
Smokers' Quitline: Tel 0171 487
3000. *Advice on stopping smoking and
details of local stop smoking support
services. Phone between 9.30 am and 5.30
pm on weekdays; recorded advice available
at other times, or write for information.*

The Association of Postnatal Illness
25 Jerdan Place, London SW6 1BE.
Tel 0171 386 0868. *Support for mothers
suffering from postnatal depression.*

LONE PARENTS

Gingerbread
35 Wellington Street, London WC2E
7BN. Tel 0171 240 0953. *Provides
advice on financial, legal and social
problems for lone parents and their
children; some local groups provide
childcare for working parents.*

Gingerbread Northern Ireland
169 University Street, Belfast BT7
1HR. Tel 01232 231147

Gingerbread Scotland
Maryhill Community Hall, 304
Maryhill Road, Glasgow G20 7YE. Tel
0141 353 0989

Gingerbread Wales
16 Albion Chambers, Cambrian
Place, Swansea SA1 1RN. Tel 01792
648728

**National Council for One Parent
Families**
255 Kentish Town Road, London
NW5 2LX. Tel 0171 267 1361.
*Research and lobbying to improve every
aspect of life for lone parent families.*

RELATIONSHIP PROBLEMS

British Association for Counselling
1 Regent Place, Rugby CV21 2PJ. Tel
01788 578328

Family Mediation (Northern Ireland)
76 Dublin Road, Belfast BT2 7HP. Tel
0232 322914

Family Mediation (Scotland)
127 Rose Street, South Lane,
Edinburgh EH2 5BB. Tel 0131 220
1610

Family Mediation (Wales)
33 Westgate Street, Cardiff, South
Glamorgan, CF1 1JE. Tel 01222
229692

National Family Mediation
9 Tavistock Place, London WC1H
9SN. Tel 0171 383 5993

Relate
Herbert Gray College, Little Church
Street, Rugby CV21 3AP. Tel 01788
73241. *Confidential counselling on
relationship problems of any kind.*

Marriage Guidance (Scotland)
105 Hanover Street, Edinburgh, EH2
1DG. Tel 0131 225 5006. *See above.*

FURTHER READING

Aleksander, T. (1992) *The right to be yourself*, Pitakus, London

Evans, R. and Durward L. (1984) *Maternity rights handbook*, Penguin, Middlesex

Gingerbread (1994) *Free to work*, Gingerbread, London

Kitzinger, S. (1994) *The year after childbirth*, Oxford University Press, Oxford.

MacGwire, S. (1992) *Best companies for women*, Pandora.

National Council for one parent families (1994), *Returning to work – A guide for lone parents*, London.

Parents at Work (1993), *The working parents handbook – A practical guide to the alternatives in childcare*. A Parents at Work publication, London

Parents at Work (1994), *Balancing Work and home – A practical guide to managing stress*. A Parents at Work Publication, London.

Parents at work (1994), *Returners handbook* A Parents at Work publication

Velmans, M. and Litvinoff, S. (1993) *Working mother – A practical handbook for the nineties*, Pocket Books.

Walton, P. (1990) *Job sharing – A practical guide*. Kogan Page, London.

Woodham, A. (1994) *HEA guide to complementary medicine and therapies*, Health Education Authority.

INDEX